FOR MY MUM, GILLIAN, WHO
FIRST TAUGHT ME TO COOK

NEW KITCHEN BASICS

10 ESSENTIAL INGREDIENTS, 120 RECIPES: REVOLUTIONIZE THE WAY YOU COOK, EVERY DAY

CLAIRE THOMSON

Photography by Sam Folan

Hardie Grant

QUADRILLE

CONTENTS

INTRODUCTION

My brother and I loved spaghetti Bolognese, and so did my dad. I remember Dad telling me about the spaghetti he ate in Italy with an old girlfriend, before my mum, before children, when he had ridden a beaten-up old motorbike from London to the South of France before ditching it, broken beyond repair, in a hedge and catching the sleeper train through to Rome. In my six-year-old imagination this information dovetailed with a battered black-and-white photograph of a young man in a polo-neck, standing in a city that looked very different from any I had visited; an incongruous Scotsman in search of pasta – it seemed so glamorous.

At the time he told me this story, we lived in Botswana. My brother and I were born in Zimbabwe and my parents met and married in Sydney, Australia. Sierra Leone, Mozambique, Seychelles, New Zealand, Germany and even the Isle of Wight all featured in the tales Mum and Dad told the two of us about the various countries where they had lived and travelled. It is of little surprise, then, compounded no doubt by the awe I had for my parents, that spaghetti Bolognese was one of my most anticipated childhood meals. I am sure that my mum, if asked, would agree that she cooked this dish nearly every week, all year round. Yet it still felt like an exotic, international supper. This was the 1980s – and from that point onwards (everywhere that I spotted it, in any case), spaghetti was invariably served as a nude tangle, with the sauce (fine dice of carrot, glossy rich red-brown) piled on top with plenty of grated Cheddar cheese. I don't think we were a sauce-mixed-through-the-pasta type of family (nevermind Parmesan!) until my teenage years. This was likely around the time that we – for I was also cooking at home by now – began to eat pasta dishes that didn't always end in Bolognese; leeks, ham, crème fraîche, with tagliatelle no less, became the new go-to. A brave new world was wolf-whistling.

Food must be in my chromosomes, as it provides the essential ingredients for how I form memories. Meals are the pivot by which I remember the other stuff of life. I can pinpoint flavours, dishes and recipes in almost all of my memories, from way back. The barbecue we had in the Kalahari Desert in 1986 when my dad and his friend had taken us in the back of a pick-up truck to watch Halley's Comet rip across the night sky. (I'll be 81, looking up, scanning the sky, the next time this happens.) The boiled ham, peas and potatoes cooked by my granny, which my brother and I used to hate and would stuff behind the huge dresser in the dining room; all the while, my grandfather would be whistling, sliding slim wooden ships into tall glass bottles next door in his workshop. The mashed strawberries and whipped cream in a Garfield Thermos flask (strange, these things that stick) that my friend used to bring to primary school as part of her packed lunch – so cool, so different from everyone else. Brittle, crystalline pieces of fudge bought with pocket money from the post office when on holiday in Lower Largo, Fife, Scotland. Even the Spud-U-Like baked potatoes that my big brother used to so revere when we moved to London from Africa. Also, I can vividly remember the taste of the cheese omelettes my mum would make for just the two of us when my brother had left home and my dad had gone to live another sort of life on a boat in Sri Lanka.

Fast-forward some twenty-odd years to the writing of this cookbook. We live in very different times: the landscape of food and recipe writing has changed, to the point of congestion. As a chef and food writer living in the UK, I am keen to foster my own blueprint for food and the memories it is capable of conjuring up. I'd like for my own children to have a litany of dishes, such as the Chicken Roasted with Grapes (page 25) or Kathi Rolls (page 77), Mapo Dofu (page 182) or the Lemon & Rose Rice Pudding (page 240) that they can call their own. I want these recipes to be different from the stalwarts of my youth, not because those weren't great and we didn't appreciate them – we still do. It's more that we know these recipes off by heart; they need no introduction, their status is unswerving, pretty much unshakable. I want to do the shaking.

What are the **New Kitchen Basics**? What dishes are we all so bored with cooking that they need new representation in the kitchen? If not spaghetti Bolognese, then what? In this cookbook I don't intend to trample on your favourite family recipes. Instead, like the feeling you might get from a wearing a new item of clothing – a bit snappy, more confident – these **New Kitchen Basics** are intended as a boost, a canny arsenal of recipes to arm you and your kitchen. And, with the supermarkets telling us that chorizo, noodles, nam pla and miso are all flying off the shelves, with recipes for burritos and katsu curries widespread in the food media, are we well enough equipped to navigate this gastronomic maelstrom? Do we need a collective cookery reboot? What is 'the new normal' and do we necessarily want one? I am assuming so; I certainly hear, 'I just can't think what to cook', from many people, most days.

Amid the tropes of Quick & Easy, 5 Ingredients, In Minutes… in essence, what we surely all hanker for is for food that is generous. We want recipes to throw the kitchen door wide open on the world, embracing everything that is good and grown or reared with principle, to exclude and ostracize nothing in the name of faddish eating. We want the food we cook to be economical and realistic and for the food we eat to be uncompromisingly satisfying.

I do believe there is a sense of disconnect between the food we voraciously look at and read about in the furore of modern food media, and the ingredients with which we all still faithfully fill our trolleys. Pasta, chicken, mince, tomatoes and potatoes… I give you 10 basic ingredients in this book. Anchored by the practical, I want this cookbook to give a new lease of life to your most trusted ingredients and for it to help you to flex your culinary muscle with the more unusual ingredients that have found favour in recent times.

New Kitchen Basics is a straightforward recipe directory for the contentedly greedy and the curious. It is for anyone at a loss as to what to make for dinner.

CHICKEN

New Kitchen Basics is my shot at writing a useful cookbook to spearhead the contemporary diet. Convenient, practical recipes to help redefine what we all cook at home. Grand ambitions. If anything, I'm in for a penny and gunning for the pound. Time, budget and culinary acumen will all determine the food we want to cook and eat at home. It's a bit of a tightrope, and I don't want to preach. With this in mind, the focus of this chapter is chicken. Far from ordinary, chicken is iconic. A good free-range bird, roasted whole, with blistering skin, is absolutely a thing of beauty. Adored by almost everyone I know and have cooked for, roast chicken is a seminal meal that should stop you in your tracks – knife and fork, glass of wine, empty plate – but, it should also demand just as much of your attention two more meals after the first. The leftover meat, including every last juicy, sticky scrap, however infinitessimal, is prised from the carcass and will go on to be given another lifeline in a pie, risotto, curry, braise or late-night sandwich. With the chicken long gone, and two meals down, you should be then left with a stark frame to begin work with yet again.

When people talk of the alchemy in cooking, there is no better example than there is meat stock. Bones in liquid – blip blip – a couple of hours later, and a whole new ingredient from something so previously, thoroughly, exhausted. Stock, let's use its proper cookery term here (I'm quite certain it isn't bone broth, at least it hasn't been in every restaurant kitchen I've ever worked in) is a given for me, and the way I like to cook. While not new, meat stock is an economical pivot, a kitchen basic by definition. It freezes brilliantly to use at another time in another dish and gives welcome depth and complexity to so many braises, soups and stews. The transformative cycle of ingredients through the practice of cooking and making food we eat and enjoy, is habitual, and why I so love putting on an apron and setting to work in the kitchen. I find it compelling.

More so than other meats, chicken seems to have an everyday reputation. Quick and versatile to cook with, it's an easy assumption to make that chicken is an obvious, almost compulsory ingredient to have ready and waiting at home. This, for me, is where this lackadaisical tale has to come to a halt. Good chicken costs money; its frequency at the kitchen table shouldn't be so straightforward. Supermarket displays of whole chickens, cellophane-wrapped and freakishly plump, have a price tag that gives away their wretched origin. Likewise, polystyrene trays packed tight with chicken breasts. These are a popular commodity because they are easy to prepare; nonetheless they are a shame, because I find the breast is often the most anodyne of all chicken meat. I much prefer the leg or thigh meat. Chickens reared with principle, bought whole or otherwise, should set you back a fair bit. Hence, roast chicken is a feast, a celebration we should anticipate. I can thoroughly recommend the method on page 20. Glorious, absolutely; significant always – but never everyday.

Commitment is what is needed when it comes to good, thoughtful cooking practice. Care for the ingredients you buy and the longevity these then have in the food you go on to cook is absolutely necessary. I am never casual with the food I buy – a bunch of herbs, a bag of lentils, a box of eggs, some chicken or a joint of meat. 'Waste not, want not' as a guiding principle was never more prescient. Rising food costs, with an increasing reliance on ready-made foods, even eating out for some, compressed with general work/life pressures can make day-to-day cooking a seemingly overwhelming task, demanding too much time for too little return. I write recipes for a living because I am determined to demonstrate that good food cooked from scratch is a realistic, inexpensive and, to say the least, satisfying option.

For the purposes of this book and specifically under the umbrella of **New Kitchen Basics**, I mostly recommend buying chicken thighs, also legs, wings and drumsticks, as they are considerably cheaper than breast, affording extra budget to buy better-quality meat. They also have better flavour and texture. In essence, these cuts are more forgiving to cook than breast; there is less room for error in cooking times. Cooked on the bone, meat will always be juicier. Roughly half of the recipes in this chapter will work well with the leftover meat from a whole roasted bird, and I would encourage you to use the recipes in this way. For example, the fried peach and bacon salad with leftover roast chicken is an obvious (read this as… ludicrously good) match. Likewise, the Madras and also the Curry Mee will work beautifully when made with leftover roast chicken. I'll let you know where appropriate.

Inspired by some of the kitchen's most convenient ingredients and very much with a world viewpoint in mind, my **New Kitchen Basics** for chicken are bold with taste and straightforward to prepare. With chicken as canvas, these punchy, universal recipes will shake up your repertoire and replace all those dishes that you might have grown bored with. I want to spark fresh wonder in a favourite ingredient.

Chicken – a quick word before we begin

There is one recipe in this chapter that uses chicken breast and this is required for the chicken to cook evenly in the pan. For the rest, you can use thighs and legs, and there is one other calling for wings and drumsticks. The most common and readily available cuts of chicken to purchase are whole birds, whole legs, whole thighs, whole drumsticks and whole wings. All come with their skin on. Boneless cuts include breasts, fillets and thighs, and are mostly sold skinless. In the recipes that call for boned meat, I give a weight; for the rest, I give the number of pieces required to feed 4. And before we start with the recipes proper, here is the most vital chicken recipe of all time…

Simple Roast Chicken

1 medium chicken, about 1.6kg (3lb 8oz)

unsalted butter or olive oil

½ lemon

salt and freshly ground black pepper

Preheat the oven to 220°C/fan 200°C/425°F/Gas 7. Rub the chicken all over with butter or olive oil.

Season generously with salt and pepper, both inside and out. Put the lemon in the cavity of the chicken, squeezing the juice in as you do so.

Place the chicken in a roasting tray and add about 1cm (½in) of water to the bottom of the tin.

Put the tray in the oven for between 1 hour and 1 hour 20 minutes, depending on the size of the chicken, until the juices run clear when a skewer is inserted into the densest part of the chicken's leg.

10 minutes before the end of cooking, turn up the oven temperature to the highest setting, to crisp the skin. Add a splash more water to the pan if it has dried out and keep an eye on the bird, so it doesn't catch or burn.

Remove from the oven and allow the chicken to rest for 20 minutes before carving, straining any cooking juices to serve with the carved chicken or for making gravy.

Chicken Madras

Chicken Tinga & Black Bean Tacos

Chicken Roasted with Grapes

Chicken with Dukkah Crumb
& Sweet Tomato Sauce

Spiced Persian Chicken Skewers

Chicken with Lots of Garlic, Almonds & Sherry

Three Cup Chicken

Chicken Salad with Fried Peach & Bacon

Picnic Chicken

Piri Piri Mozambique-style

Chicken Sours

Chicken Curry Mee

Five-Spice and Lemongrass Chicken

Chicken Madras

This curry recipe never fails. Sour with tamarind, smart with spice, it is a firm favourite. Do try to buy block tamarind rather than ready-made paste, which tends to be a bit salty and artificial-tasting. Simply break off as much of the tamarind block as you would like to use and place in a small bowl, covered with enough hot water to soften. Mix well and push the paste through a sieve (strainer) to remove any stones or fibrous matter. This should be a hot curry, so be bold with the chilli.

vegetable oil

2 teaspoons brown mustard seeds

1 large onion, peeled and finely chopped

30g (1oz) unsalted butter

3 cloves of garlic, peeled and thinly sliced

1 heaped tablespoon grated (shredded) root ginger

2–4 small green chillies, left whole

10 fresh curry leaves (optional)

1–2 teaspoons chilli powder (mild or hot, as you like)

2 teaspoons garam masala

1 x 400g (14oz) can of whole plum tomatoes, blended until smooth with 100ml (3½fl oz) water and a pinch of sugar

100ml (3½fl oz) tamarind liquid (prepared as above), or the juice of 1 lemon

1 teaspoon salt

8 chicken thighs, skin removed if you prefer, or 600g (1lb 5oz) leftover cooked chicken

rice, to serve

Put the oil in a frying pan over a moderate heat. Add the mustard seeds and fry for 30 seconds, until they begin to sizzle and pop. Add the onion and fry gently for about 10 minutes, until softened and lightly golden.

Add the butter, garlic, ginger, green chillies and curry leaves and fry for a further 1 minute, until aromatic. Add the ground spices and fry for 1 more minute, then stir in the tomato mixture, the tamarind and salt, and simmer for about 5 minutes, until rich and reduced.

Add the chicken thighs, cover and cook for 30–35 minutes, until the chicken is cooked through (or 8–10 minutes if using leftover cooked chicken). Check the seasoning, remove from the heat and serve with plain rice.

Chicken Tinga & Black Bean Tacos

If my childhood was filled with my mum's chicken casseroles, among other casseroles, then it's tacos for tea that proves especially popular in this household. Charring the raw vegetables in a super-hot pan is crucial for flavour, ramping up the intensity. I suggest soft corn tortillas here to build tacos at the table, but you could use the mixture to stuff enchiladas, burritos, fajitas or crunchy taco shells.

8 chicken thighs or 4 chicken legs, or 600g (1lb 5oz) leftover cooked chicken added to the sauce with the beans

vegetable oil

6 firm, not-too-ripe tomatoes

6 cloves of garlic, peeled and left whole

1 large onion, peeled and roughly chopped

1 teaspoon ground cumin

1 teaspoon hot smoked paprika

2 teaspoons dried oregano

2 bay leaves

2 tablespoons red wine vinegar or cider vinegar

small bunch of coriander (cilantro), roughly chopped

juice of ½ lime, or to taste

1 x 400g (14oz) can of black or kidney beans, drained and rinsed

salt and freshly ground black pepper

TO SERVE
soft corn tortillas, warmed

sour cream

1 avocado, sliced, or mashed with a little lime juice and salt

Quick pickled onions (see page 175)

lime quarters

If using chicken thighs or legs, season the meat well with salt and pepper. Pour enough oil into a frying pan to cover the base and place over a highish heat. Add the chicken and fry, skin-side down, for about 5–7 minutes, until browned and crisp. Turn over the chicken to cook the other side for about 2 minutes, until just coloured. Transfer to a warm plate and wipe the pan clean.

Add the whole tomatoes and garlic along with the onion and cook over a high heat for about 8–10 minutes, turning now and then, until blistered and charred. Remove half of the charred vegetables to a bowl and then add the spices, oregano and bay leaves to the pan. Cook for about 30 seconds, until aromatic, roughly mashing the vegetables as you go.

Add the vinegar and return the chicken to the pan along with 250ml (9fl oz) of water, bring to a boil over high heat, then reduce the heat so that the liquid is at a bare simmer. Cover the pan and cook for 35–40 minutes, or until the chicken is cooked through and tender.

Meanwhile, roughly chop the reserved charred vegetables; season with salt and pepper and a handful of the coriander (cilantro). Add lime juice to taste.

When the chicken is cooked, remove from the pan with a slotted spoon, transfer to a plate and set aside. Heat the sauce in the pan for a few minutes, until reduced to half its original volume. You can blend the sauce now, if you prefer, removing the bay leaves, but I keep it as it is.

When the chicken is cool enough to handle, discard the skin and bones and use a couple of forks to finely shred the meat. Return the meat to the sauce (or add the leftover roast chicken if that's what you're using) and add the beans. Heat through, checking the seasoning, before serving with tortillas, sour cream, avocado, Quick pickled onions and lime quarters.

Chicken Roasted with Grapes

Bursting with the heat from the oven, roasted grapes are a wonderfully sweet and fragrant foil for the chicken here. Seasonal sensibilities say prepare this dish in late summer or early autumn, when the grapes hang heavy on the vine. But, as we all know, grapes, like lemons and apples, are a fruit so widespread that their appeal is year-round. Use black or green grapes. Muscat are especially good.

8 chicken thighs

2 bay leaves

3 tablespoons olive oil

300g (10½oz) black or green grapes, split into small bunches

1½ tablespoons thyme leaves

2 small fennel bulbs, trimmed and very thinly sliced, or 4 celery sticks, sliced

1 teaspoon fennel seeds, toasted and lightly crushed

1 small red onion, peeled and thinly sliced

salt and freshly ground black pepper

In a bowl mix the chicken with the bay, 1 tablespoon of the oil, and ½ teaspoon of salt. Season with plenty of black pepper, then refrigerate for an hour.

Heat the oven to 220°C/fan 200°C/425°F/Gas 7.

Transfer the chicken, skin-side up, to a lined baking dish and bake for 20 minutes, until cooked at the edges.

Turn down the oven to 200°C/fan 180°C/400°F/Gas 6 and add the small bunches of grapes and thyme to the dish. Season with ½ teaspoon of salt and bake for a further 15–20 minutes, until the chicken is cooked through.

In a mixing bowl, toss together the fennel, fennel seeds and red onion with a big pinch of salt and the remaining olive oil.

Add the fennel and onion mixture to the baking dish with the cooked chicken and grapes, to soften ever so slightly, adding salt and pepper to taste. Serve immediately. Some crusty bread to mop up the juices is nice here, likewise some cooked rice or potatoes.

PICTURED OVERLEAF

Chicken with Dukkah Crumb & Sweet Tomato Sauce

This recipe came to be because, as a child of the 1980s, I thought Chicken Kiev was the apex of sophistication. It was one of my favourite suppers. I don't imagine my mum made it – I think she probably bought it from a store, as a treat, making it a most supremely luxurious dinner in my eyes at the time. I have made this version in the spirit of New Kitchen Basics. Bashing out the chicken flat makes this recipe more of a schnitzel than a Kiev, in any case.

4 skinless boneless chicken breasts

2 tablespoons plain (all-purpose) flour

1 large egg, beaten

150g (5½oz) dukkah (see below)

olive oil

seasoned yogurt (see page 54)

2 good knobs of butter

lemon wedges, to serve

salt and freshly ground black pepper

FOR THE DUKKAH (MAKES 150G/5½OZ)
75g (2½oz) sesame seeds

75g (2½oz) blanched almonds or skinned hazelnuts

3 tablespoons coriander seeds

1 tablespoon cumin seeds

FOR THE SWEET TOMATO SAUCE
15g (½oz) unsalted butter

1 onion, peeled and finely chopped

4 cloves of garlic, peeled and crushed

1 cinnamon stick

big pinch of chilli flakes, to taste

1 x 400g (14oz) can of whole plum tomatoes

small pinch of sugar

First, make the dukkah. Toast all the seeds and nuts together in a hot, dry pan until fragrant. Cool, and coarsely grind in a food processor or pestle and mortar, with salt and pepper to taste (use plenty of pepper).

Using a rolling pin, flatten out the chicken breasts between 2 sheets of plastic wrap or baking paper, until fairly evenly 1cm (½in) thick. Season with a little salt and pepper to taste.

Have 3 plates in front of you: put the flour on 1 plate, the beaten egg on another and the dukkah on the third. Dip both sides of each chicken breast in the flour, followed by the egg and finally the dukkah. Transfer to a fresh plate and refrigerate while you make the sauce.

To make the sauce, melt the butter in a small pan over a moderate heat. Add the onion and cook for about 8–10 minutes, until soft. Add the garlic, cinnamon and chilli flakes and cook for a further 30 seconds, until aromatic. Add the tomatoes with a hefty pinch of salt and the small pinch of sugar, and cook over a moderate heat for 15 minutes, until the sauce is rich and thick. Check the seasoning, remove the cinnamon stick, then add plenty of black pepper to taste. Set aside to keep warm.

Put enough olive oil in a large frying pan to cover the base and place over a moderate heat. Add 2 pieces of the chicken, and cook over a medium heat, for 3–4 minutes on each side, until golden. Add a knob of butter to the pan towards the end of the cooking time. Reserve the cooked chicken on a plate and keep warm while you cook the remaining 2 pieces.

Serve with the warm tomato sauce, a lemon wedge, and the seasoned yogurt to spoon over.

Spiced Persian Chicken Skewers

I grill (broil) these skewers, but they would be equally good on a barbecue (grill) and you could bake them in the oven if you'd rather. Serve with warm flatbreads or rice with seasoned yogurt (see page 54). A chopped salad is also good here – by which I mean whatever vegetables are looking happiest and heartiest: tomatoes, cucumbers and red onion with plenty of parsley and mint, a pinch of salt and a squeeze of lemon is a winning combination. You'll need 4 metal or wooden skewers (soaked in water, if wooden, to stop them burning).

½ red onion, peeled and finely chopped

100g (3½oz) Greek yogurt

2 pinches of saffron strands

½ teaspoon ground cinnamon

¼ nutmeg, grated

3 green cardamom pods, seeds finely ground

pinch of chilli flakes, or to taste

2 cloves of garlic, peeled and roughly chopped

1 teaspoon salt, plus extra to season

about 800g (1lb 12oz) skinless boneless chicken (thighs are best), cut into about 4cm (1½in) dice

1 teaspoon sumac, or a good squeeze of lemon juice

freshly ground black pepper

In a food processor or blender, blend the onion with the yogurt, saffron, cinnamon, nutmeg, cardamom, chilli, garlic and salt to create a marinade.

Put the diced chicken in a large mixing bowl, add the marinade and give it a good stir to ensure all of the chicken is well coated. Cover and refrigerate for 2–4 hours to marinate.

Preheat the grill (broiler) to medium–high and line a baking sheet with foil.

Thread the chicken onto skewers and cook under the hot grill for about 10 minutes, turning the skewers midway to ensure the chicken cooks evenly, until cooked through and lightly charred all over.

Remove from the grill and onto a serving plate, sprinkling with sumac or lemon juice.

Chicken with Lots of Garlic, Almonds & Sherry

Chicken and garlic are good friends; there are many recipes that celebrate their unity. This one gives your pan just enough of a workout to elevate this dish beyond the ordinary confines of a one-pot. Toasting and then blending the almonds with the bread and parsley to reintroduce to the chicken at the end of cooking gives a brilliant contrast: some of the crust sinks, all chewy, into the broth, while the rest provides a crunchy blast on top. Serve with sautéed potatoes.

8 chicken thighs

50g (1¾oz) blanched almonds, roughly chopped

olive oil

2 slices of crusty white bread, crusts removed, soft parts torn into 2.5cm (1in) pieces

small bunch of flat-leaf parsley, roughly chopped

2 garlic bulbs, cloves separated, skins left on

2 bay leaves

200ml (7fl oz) dry sherry, such as fino, amontillado or manzanilla or white wine

200ml (7fl oz) chicken stock or water

salt and freshly ground black pepper

Season the chicken well with salt and pepper.

Put the almonds in a frying pan over a moderate heat and dry-fry for 2 minutes, until golden. Remove the almonds from the pan and set aside to cool. Add enough olive oil to liberally coat the base of the frying pan and fry the bread pieces for about 3 minutes, until crisp and golden brown in parts.

Use a food processor to blend the roasted almonds, fried bread and parsley into a coarse crumb. Set aside.

Add another measure of olive oil to the frying pan and fry the garlic cloves over a moderate heat for 5 minutes, until just golden, then remove to a plate, reserving the oil in the pan.

Add the seasoned chicken to the same pan and fry for 5 minutes on either side, until a deep golden brown all over.

Return the garlic to the pan with the chicken and bay and pour in the sherry or wine, shaking the pan as you do so to help the wine emulsify with the oil.

Cook for 2 minutes to evaporate some of the alcohol, then stir in the stock or water, cover with a lid and cook for 15–20 minutes, until the chicken is cooked through.

At the last minute, add the almond crumb to the pan and barely stir to thicken the braise, keeping some of the crumbs on top for a crunchy texture. Remove from the heat and check the seasoning before serving.

Three Cup Chicken

This is a Taiwanese family classic, which I've downsized for a more domestic-friendly portion. (Three cups each of sesame oil, soy sauce and rice wine would make a considerable amount of chicken.) These three ingredients together offer an unbeatable triad for the chicken, which packs a punch and, as culinary combinations go, verges on the addictive. The basil at the end gives a sweet and fragrant smack to the finished dish.

40ml (1¼fl oz) sesame oil

3 fat slices of root ginger

12 cloves of garlic, peeled and left whole

1 shallot or small red onion, peeled and roughly chopped

2–3 small dried chillies

8 skinless boneless chicken thighs, cut into 4cm (1½in) dice, or 600g (1lb 5oz) leftover cooked chicken

80ml (2½fl oz) mirin, dry sherry or dry white wine

80ml (2½fl oz) light soy sauce

1 teaspoon caster (superfine) sugar

small bunch of Thai basil, or use Greek or ordinary basil if you can't find Thai

salt and freshly ground black pepper

boiled jasmine rice, to serve

Heat the sesame oil in a large frying pan over a moderate heat. Add the ginger, garlic, shallot or onion and chillies, and cook for about 1 minute, until fragrant.

If you're using uncooked chicken, arrange the pieces in a single layer. Cook them for 1 minute, then turn them over and cook for 1 minute on the other side, until just coloured.

Add the alcohol, soy sauce and sugar and bring to a boil. Reduce the heat, add the chicken, cover and simmer for about 25 minutes (or 8–10 minutes if using leftover cooked chicken), until the chicken is cooked (turn it a few times as it cooks) or warmed through.

Remove the pan from the heat and stir in the basil. Check the seasoning and serve immediately with rice.

Chicken Salad with Fried Peach & Bacon

This is the sort of salad to make deep into summer. It's a confident, effortless salad that proclaims, 'This is the life I live' (sitting around in the daytime eating salad and drinking wine with friends! I should be so lucky). As for me, I especially love to eat a salad that has the addition of something fried. Fried peach and fried bacon, with lettuce – right there are your yin and yang.

6–8 chicken thighs; or 600g (1lb 5oz) leftover cooked chicken

olive oil

4–6 slices of unsmoked streaky bacon, each slice cut into 5 pieces

1 red onion, peeled and finely sliced

2 or 3 ripe peaches, stoned, each peach cut into 6 slices

1 tablespoon runny honey

1 large soft round lettuce, leaves separated

small bunch of either basil, chervil, chives or tarragon, leaves picked

salt and freshly ground black pepper

FOR THE DRESSING
3 tablespoons olive oil

1 tablespoon runny honey

1 tablespoon Dijon mustard

3 tablespoons red or white wine vinegar

Preheat the oven to 220°C/fan 200°C/425°F/Gas 7. Line a baking tin with foil (this makes washing up easier). If you're using uncooked chicken pieces, arrange them in a single layer over the foil. Bake the chicken for about 45 minutes, basting 2 or 3 times during cooking, until the flesh is cooked through and the skin is crisp.

Meanwhile, add enough olive oil to a large frying pan to coat the base, and place over a moderate heat. Fry the bacon for about 5 minutes, until golden and crisp. Put the bacon to one side in a bowl, leaving the bacon fat in the pan, and put the pan back on the heat.

Add the onion to the pan and cook for about 8 minutes, until softened. Put the onion to one side with the bacon.

Add another lug of olive oil to the pan and fry the peach slices for about 1 minute each side. Add the honey and fry for another 1 minute or so, until the peach slices are nicely coloured. Set aside.

Once the chicken is cooked through and is cool enough to handle, pull the flesh away from the bone in big chunks, and add the cooked chicken or the leftover chicken (if using) to the bacon and onion in the bowl.

To make the dressing, in a small bowl, whisk together the olive oil, honey, mustard and vinegar and season with salt and pepper to taste.

Arrange the lettuce leaves on a large platter or in a salad bowl and add the chicken, bacon and onion. Add the herbs and finally the fried peaches. Drizzle the salad with the dressing and serve immediately.

Picnic Chicken

Picnics are wonderful things – so much more than speedy packed lunches. My granny was keen on winter picnics with hard-boiled eggs and a twist of salt, her default offering. And, like her (although perhaps without her verve for the great outdoors in freezing winter), I feel picnics call for more than just a sandwich. This marinade of buttermilk or yogurt spiked with paprika and chilli works wonders to keep the chicken juicy and flavoursome as it cooks; cool and then pack for a picnic of proportion.

600g (1lb 5oz) skinless boneless chicken thighs, each cut into 2 pieces

300g (10½oz) buttermilk or plain yogurt

2 cloves of garlic, peeled and crushed

1 teaspoon chilli flakes

2 teaspoons smoked paprika

1 tablespoon chopped rosemary or 1 tablespoon thyme leaves (or a combination of both)

1½ teaspoons salt

1 teaspoon freshly ground black pepper

1 teaspoon Tabasco, or your favourite hot sauce (optional)

200g (7oz) panko or other dried breadcrumbs

50g (1¾oz) Parmesan, finely grated (shredded), plus extra to garnish

olive or vegetable oil, for frying

small bunch of flat-leaf parsley, finely chopped, to garnish

lemon wedges, to serve

Mix the chicken with the buttermilk or yogurt, garlic, half of the chilli flakes and half of the paprika, rosemary or thyme leaves, 1 teaspoon of the salt, and the pepper and the Tabasco or hot sauce (if using). Refrigerate for at least 4 and up to 24 hours; the flavour will develop over time.

Combine the breadcrumbs with the remaining ½ teaspoon of salt, the Parmesan and the rest of the paprika and chilli flakes. Remove the chicken from the marinade and dredge it directly into the breadcrumbs, coating each piece well.

Preheat the oven to 200°C/fan 180°C/400°F/Gas 6.

Put about 1cm (½in) of oil into a large frying pan over a moderate heat. When the oil is hot, add the chicken pieces and fry until the breadcrumb coating sizzles and begins to colour. Cook the chicken in batches for 2 minutes on each side. Remove and place on a baking rack on a baking sheet. Place in the oven and cook for a further 10–12 minutes, until cooked through.

Remove from the oven and drain the chicken on paper towels. Sprinkle with additional Parmesan and the finely chopped parsley. Serve hot or cold with lemon wedges on the side for squeezing over.

Piri Piri Mozambique-style

Piri piri chicken is Portuguese in origin, but has a lineage that stretches through many of the southern African countries, where piri piri peppers have long grown in the wild. The riffs on recipes are as many as they are varied, but one thing they all have in common is a bold hand with these fiery-hot, diminutive chillies. My recipe has coconut milk in it, and I like to think the creamy, sweet milk affords me a sense of bravado as to how many piri piri chillies I then dare to add. It's a recipe to learn by rote; only then can you really know how hot you can go. You can bake the piri piri chicken, rather than grill (broil) it, if you prefer.

5 red bird's-eye or 3 red Thai chillies (this is a hot dish!)

6 cloves of garlic, peeled

1 teaspoon dried oregano

2 teaspoons smoked paprika

3 tablespoons olive oil

3 tablespoons red or white wine vinegar

juice of 1 large lemon or 2 limes

8 chicken thighs or 4 legs

100ml (3½fl oz) coconut milk

salt and freshly ground black pepper

In a food processor or blender, blend the chilli, garlic, oregano, paprika, olive oil, vinegar and citrus juice to a smooth piri-piri sauce, adding black pepper and salt to taste.

Season the chicken lightly with salt and place in a mixing bowl. Add half the prepared blended piri-piri sauce, along with with the coconut milk and mix well to coat the chicken. Set aside the remaining sauce for serving, then cover and refrigerate the chicken for at least 2 hours, preferably overnight.

When you're ready to grill (broil), preheat the grill to medium to high. Remove the chicken from the marinade using a slotted spoon, reserving any excess marinade in the bowl. Line a baking sheet with foil.

Place the chicken on the lined sheet under the hot grill for about 10 minutes on each side, turning the chicken 2 or 3 times during cooking and basting as you go with any of the leftover marinade from the bowl. Continue until the chicken is cooked through and charred in places.

Serve the chicken with the remaining piri-piri sauce you set aside before marinating.

Chicken Sours

The lime, orange and jalapeño flavours work together brilliantly here. The chicken 'sours' from the citrus, and is given a good thwack of jalapeño for heat and honey for stickiness. Basting is important during the cooking time to retain moistness, improve the finished glaze and to boost flavour in the cooked meat. Elbows on the table, arm yourself with a pile of paper napkins and set about your work – drumsticks and wings are tackled differently. A bowl of cooked rice on the side would be ideal.

1kg (2lb 4oz) chicken drumsticks and/or wings

1 teaspoon salt

2 small unwaxed oranges

1–2 jalapeños or other green chillies, finely chopped

3 cloves of garlic, peeled and finely chopped

2 teaspoons runny honey

2 tablespoons vegetable oil

juice of 1 juicy lime

freshly ground black pepper

Preheat the oven to 200°C/fan 180°C/400°F/Gas 6.

Season the chicken with the 1 teaspoon of salt, and with plenty of coarsely ground pepper. Place on a baking pan.

Grate the zest and squeeze the juice from 1½ of the oranges; finely slice the remaining ½ orange.

Combine the chilli, garlic, honey, oil, lime and orange zest and juice in a bowl, then brush it over the chicken drumsticks and/or wings.

Arrange the orange slices on the tray with the chicken and bake for about 40–45 minutes, until the chicken is cooked through and nicely glazed all over. From time to time stir the juices in the pan up and over the chicken wings, basting as you do so. Serve immediately.

Chicken Curry Mee

This is a Malaysian curry soup with coconut and lemongrass. Make this recipe when your spirits need lifting and your taste buds need to soar. It's fairly straightforward and the chicken stock really does make a difference to the finished soup. Slurping noodles, wide and fat and glossy, covered in sauce, is one of life's more pleasurable experiences. This recipe is a firm favourite with my family and the many extras we feed throughout the year. The more, the merrier.

vegetable oil

1 red onion, peeled and very thinly sliced

4 cloves of garlic, peeled and thinly sliced

2 tablespoons finely grated (shredded) root ginger

2 lemongrass stalks, finely chopped

500g (1lb 2oz) skinless boneless chicken thighs, cut into 4cm (1½in) dice, or 600g (1lb 5oz) leftover cooked chicken

1 teaspoon caster (superfine) sugar

1–2 red chillies, finely chopped (remove the seeds to reduce heat, if you like), plus extra (optional) to garnish

3 tablespoons curry powder (mild or hot, as you like)

1 x 400g (14oz) can of coconut milk

1 litre (35fl oz) chicken stock or water

3 tablespoons fish sauce

400g (14oz) egg noodles

big handful of bean sprouts

small bunch of coriander (cilantro), leaves picked and roughly chopped, to garnish

1 lime, cut into wedges

salt

Put enough oil in a large pan to coat the base and place over a moderate heat. Add half the onion, the garlic, the ginger and the lemongrass, and fry for 8–10 minutes or so, until softened and aromatic.

Turn up the heat to high and, if you're using uncooked chicken, add this along with the sugar and chilli and cook for a couple of minutes, until the chicken begins to just cook. Add the curry powder and stir to coat the meat.

Add the coconut milk, the chicken stock or water and the fish sauce (along with the cooked chicken, if using). Bring to a boil and simmer, covered, for 20 minutes, until the chicken is cooked. Check the seasoning, adding more salt if required.

Meanwhile, cook the noodles according to the packet instructions, and drain well.

Divide the noodles between 4 warm soup bowls, ladle over the hot chicken and plenty of the broth and garnish with the bean sprouts, coriander (cilantro), the rest of the raw onion, and extra chopped chilli (if you wish). Serve with wedges of lime for squeezing over.

Five-Spice & Lemongrass Chicken with Green Mango Salad

Lemongrass is widely available and has a tantalizing citrus flavour. Five-spice is a blend of ground spices, commonly star anise, cloves, cinnamon, Sichuan pepper and fennel seeds. Slashing the chicken thighs ensures all those spices can work their magic as the chicken cooks. For the accompanying salad, seek out a firm, unripe mango (of which there are usually many on the supermarket shelves). The raw sour–sweet salad works beautifully here with the fiery cooked chicken. By all means grill (broil) or barbecue (grill) the chicken, if you prefer.

4 cloves of garlic, peeled and roughly chopped

1 small shallot or ½ small red onion, peeled and roughly chopped

1 lemongrass stalk, roughly chopped

1 tablespoon grated (shredded) root ginger

1 tablespoon light brown soft sugar

3 tablespoons fish sauce

1 teaspoon five-spice powder

8 chicken thighs, slashed through the skin to the bone a few times

FOR THE SALAD
juice of 1 lime

1 tablespoon fish sauce

1 teaspoon light brown soft sugar

1 clove of garlic, peeled and crushed

1 unripe mango, pitted and cut into thin matchsticks

1 small shallot or ½ a small red onion, peeled and very thinly sliced

small bunch coriander (cilantro), finely chopped

1 teaspoon coarsely cracked black pepper

To make a marinade, blend all the ingredients, apart from the chicken and the salad ingredients, to a coarse paste. Toss the chicken in the marinade and refrigerate for 1–8 hours.

Remove the chicken from the fridge about 20 minutes before you plan to cook it and preheat the oven to 220°C/fan 200°C/425°F/Gas 7.

Line a baking tin with foil (this makes washing up easier). Arrange the chicken pieces in a single layer.

Bake the chicken for about 35–45 minutes, basting with any reserved marinade or cooking juices 2 or 3 times during cooking, until the flesh is cooked through and the skin is crisp. Remove from the oven and set aside to rest for 5 minutes.

While the chicken is resting, toss together the salad ingredients in a bowl with 3 tablespoons of water, until everything is evenly distributed. Adjust the seasoning if necessary. Serve the salad with the chicken and any of the tin juices.

TOMATOES

Tomatoes split my year in two. There are the few months when the sun shines hot and the days are long and this is when I will compulsively buy and eat properly ripe red, yellow, orange, green, even stripy, tomatoes. Ideally, they'll come from a greengrocer's shop or local market – better still, when given to me by a friend of a friend who just happens to have a glut (living the dream?). Refrigerated tomatoes, bought from the supermarket, however pretty they may look, just don't have the same draw for me. For a start, you can't smell their sweet, seductive scent, boxed off as they usually are in plastic. Ripe and fleshy with taut, shiny skins, tomatoes are completely sexy (a connotation I usually hate when used to describe food or wine, but sexy tomatoes? Absolutely, yes). Plump, and solo or four, six, eight to a vine and garlands, grape-sized, trailing like fairy lights, these are the jewels of summer. Intoxicating, in they go, and to pretty much everything. For breakfast, sliced on toast with slices (yes) of salted butter and a flurry of black pepper. For lunch, sliced, some flaky salt, again with black pepper, a splash of red wine vinegar, olive oil and left to mingle with some soft floozy herb of sorts for a good few minutes. This uncomplicated assembly is especially good with some cheese (not just mozzarella, I'm also talking ricotta, soft goat, ripe cow, swirling blue, even doorstop Cheddar), or ham (again, not just the expensive air-dried stuff, but also thick slices of cooked ham), fish, too, simply fried. Tomatoes like this are good with most things. Bread is also welcome here to swipe through and soak up the pale, mottled juices. Again for supper, tomatoes are roughly chopped if chubby and swollen, left whole if firm and dinky to hurl in a hot pan generous with olive oil, sliced garlic, salt, chilli flakes and dried oregano (a much underrated seasoning). You want the tomatoes to burst with a sense of place. This is their time. This is their moment. Minutes to make good. Stirred through some spaghetti or any short and shapely pasta, this is a supper to cook for the people you love, and who love you.

Romanticism gives way to a robust sense of practicality and I am ever thankful to the person responsible for mastering the canning process way back when*. Because, let's be honest, colder months weigh heavier on the soul here in the Northern hemisphere and good-quality canned tomatoes beat fresh tomatoes by some way in the long months when the sun is sluggish on the skyline. Canned tomatoes are a tonic for cool-climate cooking, bringing a ripe dollop of colour to winter's monochrome.

Tomatoes are generous, beguiling ingredients; they tell me all is well, that everything will be all right. This chapter gives both sorts, fresh and canned, a good run for their money and rejoices in their global omnipotence as an ingredient. The popularity of tomatoes in world cuisine is impressive, especially given that the domestic tomato, as we know it, didn't leave what is now Peru until at least the end of the 15th century. A tiny fruit grown in the wild, European explorers were enchanted with the plant, eagerly cultivating it on their return. Tomatoes soon caught on, bringing an exotic, fruity acidity to so many different styles of cooking in Europe and beyond. All of which, undoubtedly, makes the tomato a founding pillar of modern gastronomy. There, I said it.

*A Frenchman by the name of Nicolas Appert in around 1800. Preserving fresh food became a successful preoccupation for the French government in order to feed the soldiers (Napoleon being one of them) and ensure a nutritious diet for those on the battlefield.

New Kitchen Basics is a cookbook for those of us on the frontline of home cooking. In it I want to give new definition for the food this generation might like to cook at home, day in, day out.

An anthem to tomatoes, the recipes in this chapter underpin my fixation with the fruit that thinks it's a vegetable. I would not be the cook I am without them – both sorts, fresh and canned.

Tomato, Date & Chickpea Tagine

Tomato, Grapes, Basil & Mozzarella

Cherry Tomato Thakkali

Panzanella

Tomatoes Cooked with Cracked Wheat
& Brown Butter

Tomato Fritters with Butter Beans & Feta

Tomato Lescó

Bloody Mary Tomatoes

Tomato, Courgette and Tarragon Galette

Tomato & Brie Toasts with Honey & Walnuts

Roast Cherry Tomatoes with Baked Ricotta
& Pizzette Fritte

Ezme Salad

Tomato, Date & Chickpea Tagine

Tomatoes and dates blitzed and cooked together here with some chubby chickpeas (garbanzos) make for a mind-blowingly good sweet, sharp and fruity flavour. Like many things (cheese, wine, human beings...), this dish improves with age; it tastes better after a good rest. Make it the day before, refrigerate and reheat. It really is effortless to make. Some brown butter (see page 57) would be an excellent addition on top to serve; good olive oil is also fine and less of a faff.

2 tablespoons olive oil or unsalted butter

1 large onion, peeled and finely diced

1 x 400g (14oz) can of whole plum tomatoes

120g (4¼oz) pitted dates, halved

4 cloves of garlic, peeled and finely chopped

small bunch of coriander (cilantro), leaves roughly chopped, stalks reserved

1 teaspoon ground cumin

1 teaspoon ground coriander

1 teaspoon ground ginger

½ teaspoon ground cinnamon or 1 cinnamon stick

2 pared strips of unwaxed lemon zest, and the juice of ½ lemon

2 x 400g (14oz) cans of chickpeas (garbanzos), drained and rinsed

salt and freshly ground black pepper

TO SERVE
seasoned yogurt (see page 54)

couscous

brown butter (see page 57) or olive oil

Put the olive oil or butter in a large frying pan over a moderate heat, add the onion and fry for 8–10 minutes, until soft and translucent.

Blend half the tomatoes with half of the dates, then add the remaining tomatoes to the mixture and leave to one side.

Add the garlic, coriander (cilantro) stalks and all the spices to the cooked onions, stir and cook for 1 minute, until aromatic. Add the tomato mixture, the lemon zest and 100ml (3½fl oz) of water, season with salt and pepper to taste, and cook for 10 minutes, until thick and rich.

Stir the chickpeas (garbanzos) and the remaining dates into the tomato mixture and cook for 5 minutes to warm through. Add the lemon juice and check the seasoning. Remove the lemon zest from the mixture and discard, then remove the mixture from the heat.

Stir through the coriander leaves and serve with a dollop of seasoned yogurt and some couscous. Add brown butter or olive oil at the table.

Tomato, Grapes, Basil & Mozzarella

There are a million – more, a trillion – tricolore salads on menus and in paninis out there in the world. I add grapes to this popular combination. It's not a recipe – it's an assembly of ingredients to be relished at their seasonal best. It is nice to have tomatoes of varying size, some chopped, some sliced; likewise grapes, some whole, some halved. Pretty as a picture. Grapes and tomatoes – a *bona fide* **new kitchen basic.**

400g (14oz) tomatoes, as ripe and varied as you like, sliced or chopped

300g (10½oz) grapes, whatever colour or variety you like, some halved, some not

small bunch of basil or mint, leaves picked

3 tablespoons olive oil, plus extra if needed

juice of ½ lemon, or use a splash of red wine vinegar

about 400g (14oz) good-quality mozzarella (small or large balls)

salt and freshly ground black pepper

In a large mixing bowl, combine the tomatoes, grapes and basil or mint leaves, then season with salt and pepper to taste. Add the olive oil and lemon juice or vinegar and mix well. Add the mozzarella, tearing or slicing as you go, if using big balls. Arrange the salad on a plate and eat with crusty bread.

Cherry Tomato Thakkali

One to make when tomatoes are plentiful and cheap, this South Indian curry is especially good scooped up and eaten with warm naan, roti breads or the Keema Paratha on page 187. Serve in a combination with other curries or as a standalone, knock-out star of the show. A large frying pan with a lid is crucial to give the tomatoes enough space to cook – you don't want a swampy, soupy mess. Try to keep some form to the tomatoes, however soft, as they cook into the curry.

vegetable oil or ghee

1 teaspoon nigella seeds

1 teaspoon fennel seeds

1 teaspoon black mustard seeds

10 curry leaves (optional, but worth it)

1 large onion, peeled and thinly sliced

4 cloves of garlic, peeled and crushed

2 tablespoons finely grated (shredded) root ginger

2 small green chillies, left whole, plus 1–2 extra (optional), finely sliced, to serve

2 teaspoons curry powder (mild or hot, as you like)

1 cinnamon stick

800g (1lb 8oz) cherry tomatoes, halved (a mixture of red and yellow can look nice)

1 teaspoon salt

FOR THE SEASONED YOGURT
200g (7oz) natural yogurt

juice of ½ lemon

salt

Heat enough vegetable oil or ghee to coat the base of a large frying pan and place over a moderate to high heat. Add all the seeds and the curry leaves (if using) and fry for 1 minute, until they begin to sizzle and pop.

Add the onion and cook for 8–10 minutes, until nicely softened. Add the garlic, ginger, whole green chillies, curry powder and cinnamon stick and cook for 2 minutes, until fragrant and aromatic.

Add the tomatoes, salt and 100ml (3½fl oz) of water, cover, then cook for about 15–20 minutes, until the tomatoes are fully softened – don't stir too much, you don't want tomato sauce, you want to retain a bit of texture to the tomatoes.

Make the seasoned yogurt. In a bowl, mix together the yogurt, lemon juice and a good pinch of salt to taste, then put to one side.

Remove the tomatoes from the heat and discard the cinnamon stick. Serve with the finely sliced chillies, if using, a selection of Indian pickles, cooked rice or warm roti or naan breads, and a dollop of the seasoned yogurt.

Panzanella

Panzanella salads were one of the first things I made as a commis chef when I started cooking. Good bread, a couple of days old, soaked in tomato juices and brought together with more chopped tomatoes, basil, anchovies, grilled (broiled) peppers, and more, was transformative cooking, like harnessing the best there is and letting simplicity win over. Not a summer goes by without my making panzanella. Ripe tomatoes are essential here. It is certainly a salad of new-kitchen-basic proportions.

2 red (bell) peppers, deseeded and each cut into 4 wide strips

2 yellow (bell) peppers, deseeded and each cut into 4 wide strips

1kg (2lb 4oz) ripe tomatoes (mixture of plum and cherry, or use just the one sort)

2–3 cloves of garlic, peeled and finely chopped

6 anchovy fillets in oil, drained and roughly chopped

2 tablespoons red wine vinegar

4 tablespoons olive oil, plus extra if needed

2 large, stale ciabatta loaves or crustless sourdough, about 500g (1lb 2oz) altogether

1 tablespoon capers, salted and rinsed, or use brined

100g (3½oz) black olives, pitted and roughly chopped

large bunch of basil, leaves picked, and roughly chopped if large

chilli flakes or chopped fresh chilli, to taste (optional)

salt and freshly ground black pepper

Preheat the grill (broiler) to its hottest setting.

Place the red and yellow (bell) peppers skin-side up on a grill pan and grill (broil) for about 8–10 minutes, until completely blackened. Remove from the grill and immediately place the peppers in a bowl, then cover the bowl tightly with plastic wrap. Put to one side.

For the bigger tomatoes, slash the skin with a sharp knife and plunge each tomato into boiling water for about 10 seconds. Remove and plunge into cold water. The skins should now slip off easily. Roughly chop the skinned tomatoes, and place them in a sieve (strainer) suspended over a bowl to collect the juice. Cut any smaller cherry tomatoes in half, adding the juice to the bowl.

Season the tomato juice with plenty of black pepper and some salt. Add the garlic, anchovies, red wine vinegar and olive oil. Check the seasoning.

Roughly tear the ciabatta or sourdough into bite-size pieces and place in a large serving bowl. Add the tomato juices and the chopped tomatoes, and stir to combine.

Peel the peppers; the skin should easily slip from the flesh. Roughly chop and add to the bread and tomatoes. Add the capers, olives and basil, and the chilli, if using. Stir to combine.

Leave the mixture to sit for at least 30 minutes for the flavours to meld and the bread to absorb the juices. Check the seasoning, adding more salt, pepper and olive oil, if necessary, before serving.

Tomatoes Cooked with Cracked Wheat & Brown Butter

Pilaf is as old as time. Well, certainly as old as things cooked in pots over fire. For me, and the way I like to cook at home, a pilaf is the thrifty, versatile one-pot that gets cooked with reassuring frequency. With the main principle mastered – grains, liquid, heat – you can add pretty much anything you like to a pilaf. Brown butter to serve is essential, lubricating the spiced and fragrant grains; it is also a wonderful foil for the yogurt.

30g (1oz) unsalted butter

2 onions, peeled and finely diced

4 cloves of garlic, peeled and finely sliced

2 cinnamon sticks

½ teaspoon ground allspice

½ teaspoon Turkish chilli flakes, plus extra to serve (optional)

½ teaspoon salt, plus extra to season

1 x 400g (14oz) can of chopped plum tomatoes

240g (8½oz) coarse bulgur wheat, soaked in water for 10 minutes, then drained

2 bay leaves

500ml (17fl oz) chicken stock or water

brown butter (see right)

small bunch of mint, dill or flat-leaf parsley, leaves picked and roughly chopped

seasoned yogurt (see page 54), to serve

freshly ground black pepper

Melt the butter in a medium pan over a moderate heat. Add the onions and fry for 8–10 minutes, stirring occasionally, until the onions have softened. Add the garlic and cook for 2 more minutes. Stir in the spices, the ½ teaspoon of salt, the tomatoes and 100ml (3½fl oz) of water and simmer for 10 minutes, until rich and thick.

Add the bulgur wheat to the tomato mixture, along with the bay and the stock and bring to a boil. Cover, reduce the heat to low, and simmer gently for 15–20 minutes, until the bulgur is tender and the stock has been absorbed.

Remove from the heat and fluff up the pilaf with a fork. Spoon over the brown butter, top with the chopped herbs and serve with the seasoned yogurt. Some additional chilli flakes are always good, too.

Brown butter

Melt some butter (salted or unsalted, it doesn't really matter) in a small frying pan over a moderate heat. Stir from time to time and watch carefully as the butter begins to melt and the curds fall away to the bottom of the pan. You want these curds to cook to a gentle nutty brown, not too dark. Remove from the heat. You can add a squeeze of lemon, if you like. It will bubble up if you do, just be careful. Season with salt if using unsalted butter. Remove from the heat and spoon over pretty much everything; it really is that good!

Tomato Fritters with Butter Beans & Feta

I like to imagine myself making these little fritters for lunch, padding about barefoot in the cool of a kitchen, my eyes not quite acclimatized from all the sun. Outside, the bleached walls and turquoise waters give out a stark and beautiful light. There is just a ripple of a breeze; we are somewhere in Greece and it is very hot outside. So transportive are the flavours and, crashing back to Earth, I can also just as easily see myself making these for lunch one day in Bristol, England. Radio on, maybe some Nina Simone. You're welcome!

olive oil

1 bunch of spring onions (scallions), trimmed and finely sliced

4 cloves of garlic, peeled and finely chopped

600g (1lb 5oz) ripe tomatoes, finely chopped (regular or cherry tomatoes, or a mixture, are fine)

120g (4¼oz) sun-dried tomatoes, finely chopped

1 teaspoon red or white wine vinegar

good pinch of ground cinnamon

small bunch of flat-leaf parsley, leaves picked and finely chopped

½ teaspoon dried oregano

1 x 400g (14oz) can of butter (lima) beans, drained and rinsed

about 100g (3½oz) feta cheese

½ small bunch of mint or dill, leaves picked and finely chopped

150g (5½oz) plain (all-purpose) flour, plus extra if needed

1 teaspoon baking powder

vegetable oil, for frying

salt and freshly ground black pepper

Put enough olive oil in a frying pan to coat the base and place over a moderate heat. Add half the spring onions (scallion) and half the garlic and fry for about 5 minutes, until soft.

Add 100g (3½oz) of the fresh tomatoes and 1 tablespoon of the sun-dried tomatoes, along with the vinegar, cinnamon, half of the parsley and the dried oregano, and cook for 5 minutes over a moderate heat to a thick, rich sauce.

Stir through the drained and rinsed beans and season to taste with salt and pepper. Cook for a few minutes for the flavours to meld, then remove from the heat and crumble over the feta cheese. Put to one side somewhere warm.

In a large bowl, mix the remaining tomatoes, sundried tomatoes, spring onions, garlic and parsley together. Add the herbs and season to taste.

Combine the flour and baking powder in a small bowl, and gently mix them into the tomato mixture, until you have the consistency of a thick batter.

Heat about 4cm (1½in) of oil in a large frying pan over a moderate to high heat. When the oil is hot, drop tablespoons of the batter into the pan in small batches and fry for about 2 minutes on both sides, until golden. Remove the fritters with a slotted spoon and set aside to drain on paper towels. Work in batches, keeping the cooked fritters somewhere warm while you cook the rest. Serve with the still-warm beans. (Or, eat as you go!)

Tomato Lescó

This is a Hungarian dish, a bit like a goulash, where the nation's favourite trio – tomatoes, peppers and paprika – are given star billing. I've used ripe tomatoes, but you could use plum from a can, drained of their juice, when fresh tomatoes are out of season. If you want to keep this vegetarian, omit the bacon and chorizo – there is plenty of flavour to be getting on with in the mix. Boiled waxy potatoes to sit alongside, lingering in the cooked juices, are a fine match.

olive oil

2–3 slices of streaky bacon, finely chopped (optional)

100g (3½oz) chorizo or Hungarian smoked sausage, thinly sliced (optional)

1 large onion, peeled and thinly sliced

5 long romano peppers or use 3 fat red (bell) peppers, deseeded and finely sliced

5 large ripe tomatoes or 1 x 400g (14oz) can of whole plum tomatoes drained of juice

3 cloves of garlic, peeled and thinly sliced

1 teaspoon caraway seeds

2 tablespoons sweet unsmoked paprika

100g (3½oz) sour cream

small bunch of dill, roughly chopped

salt and freshly ground black pepper

Put enough oil in a large casserole dish to coat the base and place over a moderate heat. (You can be more generous with the oil if you're leaving out the bacon and chorizo.) Add the bacon and chorizo and fry, until the fat begins to exude. Remove the bacon and chorizo using a slotted spoon, leaving the fat in the dish. Put the meat to one side on a plate.

Return the dish to the heat, lower the heat slightly and add the onion and peppers. Cook for about 15 minutes, stirring occasionally, until soft.

While the peppers are cooking, if using fresh tomatoes, peel the skins using a sharp peeler if the skins are especially taut. Alternatively, slash each tomato lightly with a sharp knife and plunge into boiling water for 10 seconds, remove the skins when cool enough to handle. Quarter the tomatoes and remove the inner seeds and pulp. Roughly chop the peeled tomato flesh or the drained canned tomatoes.

Add the garlic, caraway and paprika to the softened peppers and cook for 30 seconds until fragrant, add the chopped fresh or canned plum tomatoes and cook for 5 minutes, until thick.

Add 100ml (3½fl oz) of water to the dish and season with salt and pepper to taste. Cover with a lid and cook for about 10 minutes for the flavours to meld.

Return the cooked bacon and chorizo to the dish and mix well. Add 1 heaped tablespoon of the sour cream and stir through to combine. Serve at the table with the remaining sour cream and the chopped dill for people to help themselves. Serve with boiled potatoes.

Bloody Mary Tomatoes

A well-fashioned Bloody Mary can be, to my mind, more of a meal than a drink. I rather like serving the classic Bloody Mary combination as a salad, to give a jolt to the senses and to whet the appetite. The flavours are invigorating, a non-negotiable blend of sweet, sharp, salty and fiery. The sherry in the mixture flatters the salad no end. You could use vodka, but I think you're encroaching more on cocktail territory if you do. Serve with a steak or some grilled prawns (shrimp), or as a ballsy first course.

1 small red onion, peeled and finely diced

3 tablespoons sherry vinegar or red wine vinegar

500g (1lb 2oz) ripe tomatoes, roughly diced

2–3 pale inner celery stalks, including pale leaves, finely sliced

½ cucumber, peeled, halved, deseeded and sliced

small handful of pitted green olives, roughly chopped

1–2 tablespoons horseradish, to taste (freshly grated/shredded would be best, or use creamed)

1 teaspoon Worcestershire sauce

½–1 teaspoon Tabasco or other hot sauce (add more or less to taste)

1 teaspoon Dijon mustard

½ teaspoon celery salt (optional, but worth it)

50ml (2fl oz) olive oil

2 tablespoons sherry (optional, but again, worth it)

salt and freshly ground black pepper

In a small bowl, combine the onion and vinegar, and put to one side for 10 minutes, tossing the mixture often.

Combine the remaining ingredients together in a large salad serving bowl and season with pepper and perhaps some more salt (remembering the olives and celery salt will add seasoning). Stir through the macerated onions and leave for a further 30 minutes or so (even up to a couple of hours is good), to allow the flavours to develop. Serve.

Tomato, Courgette & Tarragon Galette

Sounds swish, but really isn't. This is an elegant free-form tart with no pastry-shaping heartache. Make the pastry or buy it; no-one will be able to tell! It's the combination of tomatoes and courgettes (zucchini) that makes this dish such a pretty offering. It goes without saying that you should use ripe tomatoes, and be generous with the pepper. Departing from the usual egg-custard filling for a quiche or tart makes this galette especially straightforward to assemble. A green salad alongside would be good.

30g (1oz) unsalted butter

1 small red onion, peeled and thinly sliced

1 tablespoon thyme leaves

plain (all-purpose) flour, for dusting

300g (10½oz) shortcrust pastry

100g (3½oz) Cheddar cheese, coarsely grated (shredded)

small bunch of tarragon, leaves picked

1 small firm courgette (zucchini), thinly sliced

250g (9oz) small to medium tomatoes, thinly sliced (a mixture of colours and sizes is nice)

olive oil

pinch of sugar

1 egg yolk, beaten, to glaze

salt and freshly ground black pepper

Melt the butter in a medium frying pan over a moderate heat. Add the onion, season generously with a big pinch of salt and black pepper, and cook for 8–10 minutes, until soft and just beginning to colour. Remove from the heat and stir in the thyme.

Lightly flour a work surface and roll out the pastry to rough circle about 3mm (⅛in) thick and 30cm (12in) diameter. Transfer to a baking sheet lined with baking paper and coarsely grind black pepper over the top, giving the pastry a final roll with a rolling pin to press the pepper into the dough.

Spread the cheese over the pastry, leaving a 4cm (1½in) border around the edge. Add the onion mixture in an even layer, then layer on the tarragon, saving a few leaves for garnish, and courgette (zucchini), sprinkling with additional salt and pepper.

Add the tomato slices and drizzle with olive oil, sprinkle with a little extra salt, pepper and a tiny pinch of sugar to season the tomatoes. Fold the edge of the pastry over the tomatoes, leaving the centre open.

Brush the crust with the beaten egg, then chill the tart for 15 minutes or so, to rest. Meanwhile, preheat the oven to 190°C/fan 170°C/375°F/Gas 5. Bake for 40–50 minutes, or until the pastry is crisp and golden in places and the tomatoes are cooked and just beginning to colour.

Remove from the oven and allow to cool for 5 minutes before sprinkling over the reserved tarragon, slicing and serving. The tart can be quite fragile.

Tomato & Brie Toasts with Honey & Walnuts

Cheese on toast; tomatoes, too. A predictably delicious combination. It's the sort of simple recipe that gives cookbooks bad press. Easy to assemble, this cheese on toast is unforgettable and more than worthy of the name new kitchen basic.

4 slices of good bread (sourdough or ciabatta is good here), toasted

30g (1oz) unsalted butter

250g (9oz) ripe Brie, cut into smaller pieces

50g (1¾oz) shelled walnuts, roughly chopped

1 tablespoon thyme leaves

400g (14oz) ripe tomatoes, thickly sliced or diced as you like

2 tablespoons runny honey

salt and freshly ground black pepper

Preheat the oven to 180°C/fan 160°C/350°F/Gas 4. Butter the toasted slices of bread and place the slices on a baking sheet. Evenly distribute the Brie, walnuts and half the thyme onto each of the toasts. Bake in the hot oven for 2–3 minutes, until the Brie begins to melt a little and the walnuts start to toast.

Remove the toasts from the oven and top with the tomatoes. Season with salt and pepper, drizzle with the honey and remaining thyme and serve immediately.

Roast Cherry Tomatoes with Baked Ricotta & Pizzette Fritte

This is my favourite sort of eating: convivial, exciting food you want to serve as part of a great big shared lunch or supper. The pizza dough is easy to make; frying the dough in a pan rather than cooking it in the oven brings new texture to an old favourite. As for the baked ricotta and tomatoes: pretty as a picture. Serve the two separately, to scoop up with torn pieces of the pizzette fritte, or pile the cooked tomatoes onto the cooked ricotta and let the juices seep through the baked cheese for 10 minutes before serving. Up to you.

175g (6oz) plain (all-purpose) flour

½ teaspoon salt

100ml (3½fl oz) warm water

about 4 tablespoons olive oil, plus extra for brushing

1 teaspoon fast-action dried yeast

500g (1lb 2oz) ricotta

1 egg, beaten

2 tablespoons finely grated (shredded) Parmesan, plus extra to serve

small bunch of soft herbs (such as oregano, marjoram or basil), finely chopped, or 1 tablespoon dried oregano, plus extra for the pizzette

500g (1lb 2oz) cherry tomatoes, halved (or use larger ones, quartered)

4 cloves of garlic, peeled and crushed

1 tablespoon runny honey

flaky sea salt (optional)

dried oregano (optional)

salt and freshly ground black pepper

In a bowl, mix together the flour, salt, water, 1 tablespoon of olive oil and the yeast to form a dough. Tip out onto an oiled worktop and knead for a good few minutes, until the dough is smooth and elastic. Put the dough back in the bowl, cover with a cloth and leave somewhere warm for 45–60 minutes, to rise until just about doubled in size.

Preheat the oven to 190°C/fan 170°C/375°F/Gas 5. Brush olive oil over the base and sides of a baking dish large enough to house the ricotta mixture.

Mix the ricotta with the egg, Parmesan and half the herbs. Season with salt and pepper to taste. Spoon the mixture into the prepared dish, spread out in an even layer, and bake for about 30 minutes, until puffed in the middle and browning in places. Remove from the oven and keep somewhere warm.

While the ricotta is baking, cook the tomatoes. Mix the tomatoes with 1 tablespoon of olive oil, the garlic and the honey and season with salt and pepper. Spread out in a snug-fitting oven dish and roast for about 30 minutes, until juicy and bubbling. Remove from the oven, sprinkle over the rest of the herbs, and set aside somewhere warm.

Divide the dough into 4 equal-sized balls. Roll out each dough ball on an oiled worktop until you have 4 discs about 20cm (8in) in diameter each.

Heat a large frying pan over a high heat until very hot. Add 2 tablespoons of olive oil and have some kitchen tongs at the ready. Use your tong or hands to carefully lower one of the dough discs into the hot oil, starting closest to you and placing it away from you in case any of the oil splashes.

Use the kitchen tongs to press the centre of the dough down as it bubbles up and away from the pan. Cook the first side for about 1 minute, or until golden brown. Then, use the kitchen tongs to carefully flip the dough and cook the other side for about 1 minute. Remove the pizzetta fritta from the pan and set aside to drain on paper towels. Repeat the process with the rest of the dough discs. It's nice to scatter the cooked fritte with extra salt and some dried oregano when they come out of the pan.

Serve the pizzette fritte with spoonfuls of the baked ricotta and tomato. You might want an extra dusting of Parmesan, too.

PICTURED OVERLEAF

Ezme Salad

I love chopped salads. You know that the maker of the salad has taken the time and care to chop all the ingredients to the same size. Magic comes in a mouthful of different textures and tastes, crafted as they all are in a similar size, and creating a riot of flavour. This Turkish 'ezme' translates as 'crushed', so think pomegranate-seed size when you begin chopping your other ingredients. Give the final salad a good mix, almost crushing the ingredients with the back of a spoon as you stir, to extract as much flavour as you can.

4 large ripe tomatoes, finely diced

1 green (bell) pepper, deseeded and finely diced

1 small red onion, peeled and very finely chopped

1 clove of garlic, peeled and crushed

½ bunch of flat-leaf parsley, leaves removed and finely chopped

good pinch of chilli flakes

½ teaspoon sumac (optional, but recommended)

generous pinch of dried mint or dried oregano

juice of ½ lemon

3 tablespoons pomegranate molasses, or use the juice of 1 pomegranate mixed with 1 tablespoon runny honey

3 tablespoons olive oil

seeds of 1 pomegranate

handful of shelled walnuts, finely chopped (optional)

salt and freshly ground black pepper

Put the tomatoes, (bell) peppers and onion into a large mixing bowl. Add the garlic, parsley, chilli flakes, sumac and dried herbs.

Dress with the lemon, the pomegranate molasses and the olive oil and check for seasoning, adding salt and pepper as necessary. It's crucial to let the salad sit and rest for at least 30 minutes before serving, to allow the flavours to combine.

Before serving, add the pomegranate seeds and the walnuts, if using, and give the salad another good mix.

EGGS

'Put an egg on it.' The Urban Dictionary suggests that this phrase is rather rude and demanding. I certainly think my mother would be shocked. For her and, I imagine, many others, 'putting an egg on it' is the sensible, economic way to embellish a dish where something is missing or in need of more sustenance. In fact, in my own cooking, I have found an egg works on most things. Lentils and beans – put an egg on it. Salad of so many sorts – put an egg on it. Pizza – put an egg on it. Rice and noodles – put an egg on it. Burgers and grilled meat – do it. Smoked fish… and so on. Eggs are indispensable to the kitchen, breakfast, lunch and dinner; capable of being both the most unassuming ingredient and yet the crowning glory to so many dishes.

Principally, eggs love butter, and this happy union will always get an egg dish, however humble, off to a good start. I find eggs particularly irresistible because of their culinary malleability. There's not much they can't do. Boiled whole for the top of the shell to be lopped off, and the plump, tender yolk pierced with trim fingers of hot buttered toast – this is formative, ritualistic eating for the very young to the very old. Beaten, then cooked as voluptuous curds for scrambled eggs, or cooked as an omelette, smooth and pillowy, like an expensive eiderdown; either format serves as a fine meal, made in minutes. Frying an egg until the edges turn lacy like a swanky pair of knickers, the white opaque and glossy as Perspex, makes me smile and think back to a summer spent cooking breakfasts in a café in Sydney. The sunny-side-uppers definitely had a brighter disposition than the broke, 21-year-old cooking their eggs and making them coffee. Plane fares were costly, and it was time to go back home and get a job; possibly become more of a grown-up. I wanted to be a chef.

Eggs, for me, also encourage a giddy confusion of colour. Such pretty, dainty things, speckled and freckled, brown, terracotta, taupe, fawn through to icy blue, ivory white and even a palest, creamiest almost-green, egg shells are nature's marvel and the inspiration for many an interior design company, no doubt. Cracked, an egg yolk would put the Pantone classification in a scramble; so very many shades of yellow and orange.

I've written about eggs many times before. Their durability in the kitchen is second to none, and I use them often, in many ways. For the purposes of this book and the metanarrative (yup) behind **New Kitchen Basics**, I'm going to be single-minded and concentrate my efforts here on just hen's eggs. And, if you think the egg recipes in this chapter read like the index of a Dr. Seuss book, I'm glad. Researching and condensing my egg hit-list into just 12 recipes did feel a bit madcap, a little bit 'Cat in the Hat', such was the scope to cook from. I didn't choose some of the more idiosyncratic here just for their names (well, maybe a little?) – these are also some of my new favourite savoury egg recipes, and, for me, represent the guiding principle of this cookbook: uncomplicated, delicious, dependable dishes. I don't need to tell you how to boil an egg, a kitchen basic if ever there was, but I can point you in the direction of hoppers, masala omelettes and sabich sandwiches – all outstanding recipes that need fresh recognition and a new audience.

Lastly, I'm keeping eggs whole in this chapter, for if I even begin to make a start on separating yolk from white, and the many different uses each affords, this chapter will dwarf all others in this book.

Kathi Rolls

Coconut, Red Onion & Green Chilli Hoppers
with Two Sambals

Huevos Divorciados

Honey-roasted Squash, Kale, & Goat Cheese
Frittata

Masala Omelette

Quinoa Fritters with Green Goddess Sauce

Morning-After-the-Night-Before Eggs

Anglesey Eggs

Hoppel Poppel

Sabich Sandwich

Spinach & Walnut Khachapuri

Omurice Fried Rice

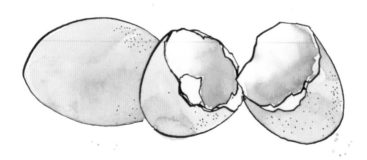

Kathi Rolls

Thought to originate in 1930s Kolkata, flatbreads, rolled and stuffed with egg and potato, among other items, were a popular grab-and-go commuter's breakfast. Kathi rolls can be as sparse or as far out as you want to make them. My version makes for a substantial, roll-able vessel to stuff chock-a-block. Do try to find chaat masala, available at most Indian grocery stores or online – it gives an indispensable fragrant, sour finishing punch to many Indian dishes.

vegetable oil

½ teaspoon mustard seeds

2 red onions, peeled and thinly sliced

½ teaspoon ground turmeric

1–2 teaspoons chilli powder (mild or hot, as you like)

1 tablespoon finely grated (shredded) root ginger

2 cloves of garlic, peeled and thinly sliced

400g (14oz) waxy potatoes, peeled and cut into bite-size pieces

4 tomatoes, finely chopped

1 lemon, halved

small bunch of coriander (cilantro), leaves picked and roughly chopped

4 large chapatis (ideally), paratha, thin naans, roti or wheat tortillas

4 eggs, each lightly beaten

2 teaspoons chaat masala, or use garam masala and a squeeze of lemon juice

salt and freshly ground black pepper

Put enough oil in a frying pan to coat the base, and place over a moderate heat. Add the mustard seeds and fry for 2–3 minutes, until they begin to pop and sizzle. Add half the onions and cook for about 5–7 minutes, until soft. Add the turmeric, chilli powder, ginger and garlic and a good pinch of salt and cook for 1 minute, until fragrant. Add the potatoes and half the tomatoes and cook for 1 minute or so, until the tomato begins to cook and thicken.

Add 200ml (7fl oz) of water, cover the pan and continue to cook for 10 minutes. Then uncover the pan, reduce the heat and cook for a further 10–15 minutes, until the potatoes are cooked through and the sauce is thick and rich-tasting. Check the seasoning and add a good squeeze of lemon juice and half the chopped coriander (cilantro), then season with salt and pepper to taste.

While the potatoes are cooking, in a mixing bowl rub a good pinch of salt into the remaining onions with your fingers, then add another squeeze of lemon and the rest of the chopped tomato and coriander.

When ready to eat, heat a non-stick frying pan over a moderate heat and add enough oil to coat the base. Add a chapati (or alternative) to the pan, pour in 1 beaten egg and spread it out evenly. Leave for about 1–2 minutes to cook on one side, then flip the egg-coated chapati over and cook on the other side until nicely coloured (don't worry if a bit of the uncooked egg mixture pours off as you flip the chapati – just scoop it back on to cook).

Remove from the pan and pile on some of the cooked spiced potato and the chopped tomatoes, along with a good pinch of chaat masala. Roll it up and serve immediately. Repeat for the remaining chapatis.

Coconut, Red Onion & Green Chilli Hoppers with Two Sambals

Coconut pancakes fried with an egg, called hoppers, are a Sri Lankan breakfast staple. Here served with two sambals – one fiery and fresh, one feathery with coconut – this is a breakfast or brunch to master and make again and again. Work quickly to shape the pancake, using a high-sided frying pan or a wok for a traditional lipped hopper. Rice flour is best, but you can get away with using plain (all-purpose) flour.

150g (5oz) fine rice flour or 100g (3½oz) plain (all-purpose) flour

200ml (7fl oz) warm water

1 teaspoon fast-action dried yeast

1½ teaspoons caster (superfine) sugar

½ teaspoon salt, plus extra to season

100g (3½oz) desiccated (shredded) coconut

200ml (7fl oz) boiling water

1 red onion, peeled and very finely diced

4 teaspoons chilli flakes

juice of 1 lime

2 teaspoons fish sauce (optional, but pretty good)

1-2 green chillies, finely chopped (remove the seeds if you want less heat)

4 tablespoons finely chopped coriander (cilantro) or mint

4 eggs

vegetable oil

First, make the batter. Mix the flour with the warm water, yeast, ½ teaspoon of the sugar and the salt. Leave to one side for about 30 minutes to start to bubble.

Meanwhile, put the desiccated (shredded) coconut into a heatproof bowl and pour over the boiling water.

To make the first sambal, put half the red onion with 3 teaspoons of the chilli flakes in a pestle and mortar and pound (or give them a quick pulse in a food processor, if you prefer) to a coarse paste. Put the mixture in a bowl and mix with half the lime juice and the fish sauce (if using), and a big pinch of salt to season. Put into a serving dish and set aside.

To make the second sambal, mix half the soaked coconut with the remaining 1 teaspoon of sugar, the remaining 1 teaspoon of chilli flakes, another big pinch of salt, 2 tablespoons of the remaining diced red onion and the remaining lime juice. Put into a bowl and set aside.

When the batter is bubbly, mix in the remaining diced red onion, the green chilli, the remaining soaked coconut and the herbs. Break 1 egg into a cup and have it ready to add to the pancake.

Heat a non-stick frying pan over a moderate heat and rub with a thin film of oil. Pour a ladleful of the batter into the pan, tilting it so the batter begins to cook up the edges of the pan in a thin layer. Quickly add the egg into the centre of the pancake and cover with a lid. Leave to cook for about 2–3 minutes, until the egg is just cooked and the edges of the pancake are starting to colour.

Run a flexible spatula or palette knife around the edges of the pan and slide the hopper onto a plate. Repeat with the remaining batter and eggs. Serve immediately with generous helpings of the 2 sambals.

Huevos Divorciados

Huevos divorciados, or divorced eggs, is a popular Mexican dish. Served in the traditional way, the two tacos, each with a fried egg, have a barrier of refried beans separating them. I don't think this wall is necessary. Instead, I like to smear each with the soft and flavourful beans, giving a nice contrast between warm taco and frilly egg. Peace not war, every time.

4 ripe tomatoes

8 cloves of garlic, 4 whole with skin on, 4 peeled and finely chopped

2 onions, peeled, 1 quartered, 1 finely diced

6 tablespoons vegetable oil

2 teaspoons ground cumin

50g (1¾oz) canned chipotle chillies in adobo, or 2 teaspoons hot smoked paprika and ½ roasted red (bell) pepper

250g (9oz) green or unripe tomatoes, or tomatillos if you can find them, chopped

2 green chillies, thinly sliced

1 teaspoon dried oregano

small bunch of coriander (cilantro), leaves picked and roughly chopped

1–2 limes, depending on juiciness

1 x 400g (14oz) can of kidney, black or pinto beans, drained and rinsed

8 eggs

8 small corn or wheat tortillas, to serve

salt and freshly ground black pepper

First, make a salsa roja (red salsa). Heat a medium pan over a high heat until hot. Add the whole ripe tomatoes, whole garlic and the onion quarters and dry-fry for 8–10 minutes, until beginning to char. Remove from the heat and cool slightly. Peel the skins from the tomatoes and garlic cloves and finely chop them together.

In a small pan over a moderate heat, add 2 tablespoons of the oil, then add 1 teaspoon of the cumin, the chipotle chillies (or paprika and pepper alternative), and the charred, chopped vegetables. Bring to a simmer and cook for about 5 minutes, until the excess liquid has evaporated and the salsa has cooked to a rich, thick sauce. Season well with salt and pepper and set aside.

Next, make a salsa verde (green salsa). Heat another 2 tablespoons of oil in a small pan over a moderate heat. Add the diced onion and half of the chopped garlic and fry for about 8–10 minutes, until softened. Add the unripe tomatoes, green chillies and oregano, bring to a simmer and cook for 5 minutes, until the excess liquid has evaporated and the salsa is thick. Remove from the heat, season with a good pinch of salt and stir in the coriander (cilantro) and the juice of ½ a lime. Set aside.

In a pan over a moderate heat, fry the remaining chopped garlic in the remaining 2 tablespoons of oil for 1 minute, until soft. Add the remaining 1 teaspoon of cumin, along with the beans, and cook for 5 minutes for the flavours to meld. Remove from the heat and season to taste with salt and pepper. Use the back of a fork to mash the beans in the pan to a coarse purée. Keep warm.

Fry the eggs (keeping the yolk runny) and warm the tortillas in a dry pan or microwave. Place 2 tortillas on each plate, smear some refried beans over each tortilla and top each with a fried egg. Spoon salsa verde over one egg and salsa roja over the other. Serve immediately.

Honey-roasted Squash, Kale & Goat Cheese Frittata

I grew up with quiche Lorraine being the default offering my mum would make to take to a party or lunch. She makes a good one. I think frittatas fill a similar gap and I have worked in countless restaurants and cafés where the lunchtime riffs on frittata have been many. You can pretty much throw anything into a frittata – a new kitchen basic.

300g (10½oz) butternut squash or sweet potato, diced (about 3cm/1¼in)

2 tablespoons olive oil, plus a splash extra to cook the frittata

1 tablespoon runny honey

30g (1oz) unsalted butter

1 large red onion, peeled and cut into 0.5cm (⅝in) rings

4 good-sized stalks of kale, stems removed, roughly chopped

7 eggs

80ml (2½fl oz) whole milk

½ teaspoon chilli flakes (optional)

100g (3½oz) goat, feta or your favourite cheese, crumbled or roughly chopped

small handful of pitted black olives

salt and freshly ground black pepper

Preheat the oven to 200°C/fan 180°C/400°F/Gas 6.

In an ovenproof baking dish, toss the squash with the olive oil, honey and a good pinch of salt and pepper and roast for 20 minutes, or until golden brown and tender.

Melt the butter in a non-stick, ovenproof frying pan (make sure it will fit in your oven) and add three quarters of the onion rings. Fry for about 8–10 minutes until tender and translucent. Add the kale and continue cooking for 5 minutes, until the kale has softened and wilted down a bit.

When the squash is ready, add it to the onion and kale and mix to combine, then remove from the heat.

Whisk the eggs and milk in a big bowl with the chilli flakes, if using, and some salt and pepper to taste. To complete the frittata mixture, add the cooked vegetables to the egg mixture and stir to combine. Wipe out the frying pan.

Add a splash more olive oil to the frying pan and turn up the heat to get the pan very hot. Pour the frittata mixture into the hot pan. Turn down the heat and top with the cheese, olives and the remaining onion rings. Place the frying pan in the hot oven for about 30–35 minutes, or until the frittata is firm to the touch and golden brown on top.

Remove the frittata from the oven and allow to rest for 5 minutes before sliding out onto a chopping board or large plate. Serve warm or cold.

Masala Omelette

Omelettes are some of my favourite and most anticipated suppers to make for others. As you crack eggs and heat the pan, in that particular moment your focus is exclusively on the person for whom you are cooking the omelette. It's a singular and quite precise pocket of time that differs from so many others in the clatter of the kitchen. Plain omelettes are excellent; masala omelettes are better. If you can't face cooking four individual omelettes, cook this as one giant omelette, with a longer cooking time, and cut into thick slices to serve.

6 eggs

1 onion, peeled and finely diced

½–1 teaspoon chilli powder (mild or hot, as you like)

small bunch of coriander (cilantro), roughly chopped

100g (3½oz) cherry tomatoes, chopped

1–2 green chillies, finely chopped (remove the seeds to reduce heat, if you like)

1 teaspoon ground turmeric

vegetable oil or butter

1 teaspoon garam masala

1 teaspoon dried fenugreek leaf (optional)

chilli sauce or ketchup, to serve

salt and freshly ground black pepper

Break the eggs into a bowl, beat and mix in the onion, chilli powder, coriander (cilantro), tomatoes, half the green chilli and the turmeric. Season to taste with salt and pepper.

Heat 2 teaspoons at a time of oil or butter over a medium heat in a large non-stick frying pan. Pour in a quarter of the egg mixture. Swirl the pan to evenly distribute the mixture. Cook for 1 minute, until just set, then fold over in half and gently cook for a further 30 seconds to 1 minute, until the omelette is just set in the middle. Slide the omelette onto a plate and keep warm. Repeat for the remaining egg, using a quarter of the mixture at a time.

Serve the omelettes sprinkled with the remaining green chilli, the garam masala and the fenugreek, if using, and with chilli sauce or ketchup on the side.

Quinoa Fritters with Green Goddess Sauce

Quinoa is a brilliant and speedy ingredient for the kitchen. Tender when cooked, with a delicate white furl of a tail, it has a nutty, satisfying taste. Mixed here with eggs, feta and herbs, and fried as a fritter, the cooked quinoa provides some welcome ballast to a dish that is bombproof. I'm a sucker for a striking name, and it doesn't come much better than Green Goddess – a pungent mayonnaise-based sauce made intensely green with masses of herbs and spring onions (scallions). I've supplemented some of the mayonnaise with yogurt to lighten the result.

200g (7oz) quinoa

100g (3½oz) shop-bought or homemade mayonnaise

100g (3½oz) Greek yogurt, crème fraîche or sour cream

big bunch of flat-leaf parsley, leaves picked and finely chopped

small bunch of mint, leaves picked and finely chopped

1 bunch of spring onions (scallions), very finely chopped

2 cloves of garlic, peeled and finely chopped

zest of 1 unwaxed lime or 1 small unwaxed lemon, plus a squeeze of juice

3 eggs

100g (3½oz) feta cheese, crumbled

1 teaspoon ground cumin

50g (1¾oz) plain (all-purpose) flour

vegetable oil, for frying

chilli flakes, to serve (optional)

salt and freshly ground black pepper

Cook the quinoa in 500ml (17fl oz) salted water for about 15 minutes, or until the water has been absorbed and the quinoa is tender. Spread out the cooked quinoa on a large plate or tray to cool.

Mix the mayonnaise and yogurt with half the herbs, half the spring onions (scallions), half the garlic and a squeeze of lime or lemon juice. Check the seasoning, adding salt and pepper to taste.

Mix the cooled quinoa with the remaining herbs, spring onions and garlic, the eggs, feta, cumin, lime or lemon zest and flour. Season with salt and pepper.

Heat about 4cm (1½in) of oil in a non-stick frying pan over a high heat. Drop tablespoons of the fritter batter into the hot oil and fry, in batches, for 3–4 minutes on each side, until golden and crisp. Keep each batch warm while you cook the remainder.

Season the fritters with a little more salt and pepper, or use chilli flakes if you like, and serve warm with the Green Goddess sauce and the leftover lime or lemon.

Morning-After-the-Night-Before Eggs

When your body feels sluggish from poor sleep, and maybe one too many the night before, what you need is a really satisfying breakfast. Something to quell a rebellious head that would really rather sink back deep down under the duvet. To those ends, make these breakfast eggs – like a bull in a china shop, this fiery panful should do the trick. Keep the yolks runny and have good crusty bread at the ready to mop.

olive or vegetable oil

150g (5½oz) cooking chorizo, sliced into coins

1 red or white onion, peeled and finely sliced

1 red (bell) pepper, finely diced

1 green (bell) pepper, finely diced

3 cloves of garlic, peeled and finely chopped

1 x 400g (14oz) can of whole plum tomatoes or in-season ripe tomatoes

4 eggs

1 tablespoon Sriracha or other hot sauce, plus extra to taste

100g (3½oz) sour cream or crème fraîche

2 large pickled jalapeños or fresh green chillies, finely chopped (optional)

small bunch of flat-leaf parsley, leaves picked and roughly chopped

salt and freshly ground black pepper

Put enough oil in a large frying pan to coat the base and place over a moderate heat. Add the chorizo and fry for about 5 minutes, until the meat is just beginning to brown and the chorizo oil has begun to run out. Remove to a plate, leaving the fat behind in the pan, and keep warm.

Add the onion and peppers to the pan and cook for about 10 minutes, until softened. Add the garlic and fry for a couple of minutes, then add the tomatoes, and cook for about 10 minutes more, until rich and thick. Check the seasoning, adding salt and pepper to taste.

Make pockets in the sauce and break an egg into each. Season the eggs lightly with salt and pepper and turn down the heat as low as possible. Distribute the cooked chorizo evenly over, cover the pan, and cook for about 8 minutes or so, until the whites of the eggs are opaque and the yolks still runny.

While the eggs are cooking, in a small bowl mix the Sriracha or other chilli sauce with the sour cream or crème fraîche. Add a pinch of salt, to season.

To serve, sprinkle the chopped chillies and parsley over the eggs in the pan and serve with the chilli sauce and sour cream mixture on the side, and hunks of crusty bread.

Anglesey Eggs

Or, to give it its Welsh name, *Wyau Ynys Mon*. For its reference point here in this cookbook, I'm turning to Jane Grigson. In her book *English Food*, this rather ordinary-sounding recipe perfectly demonstrates Grigson's skill as a cook and her flair as a food writer. To this day, her books remain timeless, with thoughtful recipes, often made with frugal ingredients, all the while skilfully woven with sublime food writing – a joy to read and cook from.

75g (2½oz) unsalted butter, plus extra for greasing

1 large leek, trimmed and finely diced

8 eggs

1kg (2lb 4oz) floury potatoes, peeled and cut into about 3cm (1¼in) squares

600ml (21fl oz) whole milk

small bunch of chives, roughly chopped, or tarragon or flat-leaf parsley, leaves picked and roughly chopped

50g (1¾oz) plain (all-purpose) flour

150g (5½oz) Caerphilly or Cheddar cheese, coarsely grated (shredded)

40g (1½oz) fresh breadcrumbs

salt and freshly ground black pepper

Preheat the oven to 220°C/fan 200°C/425°F/Gas 7 and grease a baking dish (measuring about 25 x 20cm/8 x 10in) with butter.

Melt 25g (1oz) of the butter in a large saucepan over a moderate heat. Add the leeks and fry for about 10 minutes, until soft.

Meanwhile, bring the eggs to a boil in a pan filled with cold water. When the water comes to a full boil, turn off the heat and leave the eggs in the water for 9 minutes. Remove with a slotted spoon and set aside to cool.

Cook the potatoes in salted boiling water for about 10 minutes, or until they are soft but still hold their shape. Drain well, then crush the potatoes fairly coarsely with another 25g (1oz) of the butter. When the leeks are ready, add them to the potatoes with a couple of tablespoons of the milk. Season to taste with salt and pepper.

Spoon the potato and leek mixture into the prepared baking dish. Peel and quarter the hard-boiled eggs and arrange them on top. Scatter over the chopped herbs.

Using the same pan that the leeks were cooked in, melt the remaining butter, add the flour and cook for 2 minutes. Little by little, whisk in the rest of the milk and cook until the sauce thickens and is smooth and velvety. Cook for about 5 minutes, remove from the heat, add half the cheese and season to taste with salt and pepper.

Pour the cheese sauce over the herbs. Mix the remaining cheese with the breadcrumbs, and sprinkle over the top of the sauce.

Bake for 15–20 minutes, until bubbling and golden brown. Remove from the oven and serve.

Hoppel Poppel

It's here because I like the name. Hoppel Poppel, or German farmer's eggs, like all sensible recipes is more of a method than any hard-and-fast rulebook of ingredients. You want the potatoes to crisp at the edges, but remain fudgy enough to soak up all the flavour. You want the buttery scrambled eggs to slump modestly among the spuds and bacon, and for the pan to arrive at the table giving a satisfying burp of steamy flavour. It's eggs and bacon, a bit differently.

800g (1lb 12oz) new, small, waxy potatoes, or any cooked leftover potatoes

vegetable oil

50g (1¾oz) unsalted butter

1 small white onion, peeled and finely diced

200g (7oz) diced bacon, ham or leftover roast pork

150g (5½oz) salami (or you could use diced chorizo)

small bunch of flat-leaf parsley, leaves picked and roughly chopped

8 eggs, beaten

50ml (1¾fl oz) whole milk

100g (3½oz) Cheddar cheese, grated (shredded)

4 slices of bread or 2 split bagels, toasted, to serve

salt and freshly ground black pepper

First, if you're using uncooked potatoes, cook them in salted boiling water until tender. Remove from the heat and cool slightly. Slice the potatoes (new or leftover) into fat coins.

Heat a large frying pan over a moderate heat. Add enough oil to cover the base of the pan, and fry the potatoes for about 5 minutes, until they begin to crisp and brown in places.

Add half the butter, the onion and both meats to the pan and continue cooking, stirring from time to time, for 8–10 minutes so that the potatoes continue to colour, the meat browns and the onions soften. Add the parsley and mix well.

Meanwhile, mix the eggs in a bowl with the milk and cheese. Season generously with black pepper and a good pinch of salt.

Melt the remaining butter in a medium saucepan over a medium to low heat. Pour in the eggs and scramble, until just set but still wobbly – about 3–5 minutes.

Add the scrambled eggs to the pan with the fried potato mixture and gently mix through. Remove from the heat and serve piled high on toasted bread or bagel.

Sabich Sandwich

Of all the places I'd like to wake up and eat breakfast most, it might have to be somewhere like Jerusalem. The Middle East does breakfast very well. And this is what I'd most like to eat: thick slices of cooked, creamy aubergine (eggplant), smothered in hummus, tahini and yogurt, lots of lemon, chopped salad and hard-boiled eggs, all stuffed in a warm pocket of pita bread. I would also have plenty of chilli sauce and some good, strong coffee. Aubergines are the star here together with the eggs; this is a breakfast of champions. The amba sauce is optional, but crucial if you're after a genuine sabich sandwich.

4 eggs

olive or vegetable oil, for frying

1 large aubergine (eggplant), sliced into 1cm (½in) rounds

2 ripe tomatoes, finely diced

½ cucumber, peeled, halved, deseeded and finely diced

¼ white cabbage, very thinly sliced

juice of 1 lemon

small bunch of flat-leaf parsley, leaves picked and finely chopped

50g (2oz) tahini

100g (3½oz) plain yogurt

4 pita breads

150g (5½oz) hummus

chilli sauce, to taste (use your favourite)

salt and freshly ground black pepper

FOR THE QUICK AMBA SAUCE (OPTIONAL; USE BOUGHT MANGO CHUTNEY IF YOU LIKE)
1 unripe mango, peeled, stoned and finely chopped

zest and juice of ½ unwaxed lemon

½ teaspoon cumin seeds

½–1 teaspoon chilli flakes

If you're making the amba sauce, start with this. Blend all the ingredients together in a food processor, seasoning to taste. Put to one side.

Bring the eggs to the boil in a pan filled with cold water. When the water comes to a full boil, turn off the heat and leave the eggs in the water for 9 minutes. Remove with a slotted spoon and set aside to cool.

Put 0.5cm (¼in) of oil in a frying pan over a high heat. Fry the aubergine (eggplant) in batches for about 3–5 minutes per batch, until golden and tender throughout. Transfer to a tray lined with paper towels and season with salt.

Mix the tomatoes, cucumber and cabbage with half the lemon juice and the parsley and season with salt and pepper. Put to one side.

Blend the tahini and yogurt together with a big pinch of salt and the remaining lemon juice.

Toast and split each of the pitas to open them up like pockets. Then smear the inside of each pita with the hummus, add slices of fried aubergine and drizzle with a little of the tahini sauce. Peel and slice the hard-boiled eggs, and add to the pita pockets along with some of the salad, more tahini sauce, and the amba sauce, if you've made it. Finish with the chilli sauce and eat straightaway.

Spinach & Walnut Khachapuri

This is cheese bread from Georgia, baked here with spinach and an egg. The butter on top forms a molten puddle, making these attractive gondola-shaped breads especially delicious. Baked in the traditional way, khachapuri would have enough of a lip that you can saw it off with a small knife, and then use the offcuts to dip into the runny yolk and melted cheese, before picking up the khachapuri and demolishing the rest.

500g (1lb 2oz) plain (all-purpose) or strong flour

2 teaspoons fast-action dried yeast

1 teaspoon caster (superfine) sugar

1 teaspoon salt, plus extra to season

1 tablespoon olive or vegetable oil, plus extra for frying

350ml (12fl oz) warm water

1 onion, peeled and finely diced

500g (1lb 2oz) spinach, use cooked fresh or defrosted, either way squeeze out the water

150g (5½oz) mozzarella or halloumi cheese, chopped or grated (shredded)

5 eggs

40g (1½oz) unsalted butter

40g (1½oz) shelled walnuts, roughly chopped (optional)

freshly ground black pepper

Mix the flour, yeast, sugar, salt, oil and water together in a large mixing bowl, until well combined to a soft dough. Turn out onto a lightly floured or oiled surface and knead for a few minutes until elastic and smooth to the touch. Put back in the bowl, cover with plastic wrap and put to one side until almost doubled in size (about 2 hours).

Preheat the oven to 220°C/fan 200°C/425°F/Gas 7. Line a baking sheet with baking paper, or, better still, heat a pizza stone in the oven.

Put enough oil in a frying pan to coat the base, and place over a moderate heat. Add the onion and fry for 8 minutes or so, until soft. Stir through the spinach and season to taste with salt and pepper. Turn off the heat and allow to cool slightly, then stir through the cheese.

Divide the dough into 4 balls and roll each into an oval shape about 25cm (10in) long. Divide the spinach mixture between the pieces (at this stage it helps to leave an indent in the spinach to add the egg later), leaving a 3cm (1¼in) border all around the edge. Fold up the sides and pinch the ends to seal.

Lightly beat 1 of the eggs in a bowl to make a glaze, and brush over each dough shape before gently placing them on the lined baking sheet or pizza stone. Bake for about 5 minutes, until the dough is beginning to brown in places underneath. Crack an egg into the centre of each dough shape and add a good-sized knob (about 2 tablespoons) of butter. Place back in the oven and continue cooking until the egg whites are opaque and the dough is cooked through.

Remove from the oven, sprinkle with the walnuts and serve immediately.

Omurice Fried Rice

Fried rice, in my book, is a surefire new kitchen basic. Like having your cake and eating it, this Japanese recipe combines the skill and covetous wobble of a well-made omelette with the indulgent comfort of fried rice. With the barely set omelette draped languidly over the rice, you won't be able to help but slash the omelette with a knife, enabling the runny egg to begin its descent into the rice beneath. The tomato ketchup and soy sauce combination is authentic and knockout.

4 tablespoons ketchup

1 tablespoon soy sauce

vegetable oil

350g (12oz) short-grain or sushi rice, cooked and cooled, or use leftover cooked rice

1 small onion, peeled and finely diced

200g (7oz) boneless chicken or leftover cooked chicken, diced

2 spring onions (scallions), thinly sliced

4 large eggs, lightly beaten

salt and freshly ground black pepper

Mix the ketchup in a small bowl with the soy sauce and 1 tablespoon of water.

Heat a wok or frying pan until it is very hot. Add a good measure of oil and fry the cooked rice over a high heat for about 4 minutes, until the rice begins to go light brown and toasted in parts. Transfer to a bowl.

Add another measure of oil to the same wok or frying pan. Place over a high heat and add the onion. Fry for about 3 minutes, until just softened, then add the chicken (raw or leftover) and stir-fry for about 5 minutes, until cooked and beginning to brown, or heated through.

Return the rice to the pan and toss together with half the ketchup mixture and all the spring onions (scallions). Scrape the mixture into a small warm bowl, squashing it down firmly.

Place a plate on top of the bowl and, holding both plate and bowl, invert so that the bowl is sitting upside-down on top of the plate. Keep warm.

Season the beaten eggs, then heat 1 tablespoon of oil in a frying pan over a moderate heat. Add the beaten eggs and stir rapidly with a spatula, while shaking the pan to agitate the eggs as the omelette forms. Do not over-cook the omelette, you want it to be creamy and barely set within.

Lift the bowl off the rice, leaving the rice in a firm mound. Slide the very wobbly omelette on top of the dome of cooked rice and serve immediately with the remaining ketchup mixture.

SALAD & VEGETABLES

You don't have to be a vegetarian to eat vegetables. Recent years have seen something of a sea change in attitudes to vegetarian and vegan eating, with some industry-wide initiatives championing vegetables and salads as the more critical ingredients to a dish, where previously meat, fish or dairy might have been given the limelight. I don't think I am imagining this. Food bubbles are easy to burst, given enough impetus. Online and print food media do seem to be showcasing edible plants in a way they haven't done previously. Ignore the marketing monikers of so-called superfoods or even such things as 'courgetti', where vegetables have been whittled to ape an alternative (cauliflower steak, anyone?), disguising their vegetative make-up, duping our subconscious into thinking what we're actually eating is our preferred starchy or meaty option.

I say don't bother. Vegetables don't need any marketing spiels or gadget wizardry; they are great just as they are, all shapes and sizes. Prepared or cooked with flair and creativity, eating a largely plant-based diet is easy, to say the least, and a delicious way of life.

To help with this, it's important we make vegetables and salads worthy of the same fervour with which we approach a battered fillet of fish or beef burger stuffed in a bap. Pulses, grains, cans of tomatoes, olive oil and plain yogurt seem to make up the mainstay of my weekly shopping. All of which are combined and cooked with an emphasis on vegetables, which is how I like to cook for my own family; it is also a considerably cheaper way to shop. I live in a city near three fantastic fruit and vegetable shops, where quite often they will have various vegetables bagged up on sale at silly prices. They want these gone to make room for more. Retail – especially, it would seem, in the perishable world of fruit and vegetables – is fast-turning and fickle. Someone may have over-ordered, or perhaps cauliflower is having more of a moment than broccoli – it can vary widely. The (bell) peppers might be grouped more green than red or yellow to compensate as the more unfashionable of the trio, or the mushrooms might be workhorse button rather than the fancy Portobello variety. I love this knock-down lottery, spilling out onto the pavement, and what I cook at home is often determined by this most unprepossessing display.

In addition to these get-gone-quick stands is the usual seasonal bounty common to all greengrocer stores. In cold months these stores tend to have a very green-brown-beige, earthy hue; in summertime, a riot of colour and crunch. I find cooking much quicker come the summer months, and sometimes the best sorts of summery dishes are just a collision in a salad bowl. Wintertime cooking calls for more layers; like with your favourite jumper or cardigan, you just need to add more to keep warm and bonny.

New Kitchen Basics as a principle or rule of conduct has its toughest job to do here in this chapter. I want to encourage a new and practical manifesto for the home cook. One where vegetables and salads are no longer an afterthought or a supporting side dish to more expensive chunks of protein, but the backbone or showstopper of the entire meal. I am at my happiest in the kitchen, apron on, faced with a pile of vegetables to make good, make dinner, make anything.

They are the primary context by which I like to cook; they are my default setting. I will always think first of what vegetables or salads I would like to use, then build a meal around those. I have worked the grill (broiler) section in many restaurants, but put me on sides (where the pasta or the vegetables tend to get cooked), or even on starters (assembly jobs: mostly small-scale attractive dishes, less demonstrative of stove work) – this is the kind of cooking where I best thrive.

I love the nuance of using vegetables and salad ingredients in the dishes I make; I think these ingredients demand more intuitive skill in the kitchen. And those with telltale green fingers are often the better cooks.

Just 12 recipes here, a mere snapshot of where, and with what esteem, I place the green stuff.

Spiced Roasted Courgette with Lime,
Avocado & Broken Tortilla

Slaw

Broccoli, Roast Onion & White Beans
with Anchovy Butter

Rojak Salad of Bean Sprouts, Cucumber,
Cabbage & Peanuts

Fennel, Red Onion, Olive, Orange
& Pistachio Salad

Gem, Sprout & Hazelnuts with Chives
& Creamy Dressing

Sweet Potato with Roast Corn, Black Beans
& Coriander

Mattar Paneer

Apricot, Cauliflower & Pine Nut Tabbouleh

Green Salad for Now

Jalfrezi Peppers with Chickpeas & Coriander

Green Beans with Tomato, Turmeric
& Spiced Butter

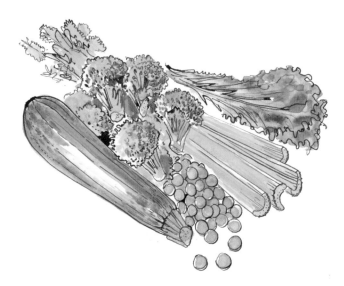

Spiced Roasted Courgette with Lime, Avocado & Broken Tortilla

Perhaps my favourite of the salads and vegetables in New Kitchen Basics, this recipe ramps up flavour and texture in robust combination. Courgettes (zucchini) served like so are more va-va-voom than you might ever have cooked or eaten them before. Serve this on its own as a light lunch or in tandem with an assortment of barbecue (grill) dishes. I would be very happy eating this with a very cold glass of beer, maybe sand between my toes... mariachi band optional.

4 courgettes (zucchini), diced

vegetable or olive oil

1–2 teaspoons hot smoked paprika or chipotle chilli flakes

1 teaspoon ground cumin

3 cloves of garlic, peeled and finely sliced

80–100g (3–3½oz) tortilla chips, broken up

2 avocados, flesh cut into bite-size pieces

100g (3½oz) feta cheese, crumbled

small bunch of coriander (cilantro), roughly chopped

1–2 green chillies, finely sliced (optional; remove the seeds to reduce heat, if you like)

1 lime, cut into wedges, to serve

salt and freshly ground black pepper

Preheat the oven to 220°C/fan 200°C/425°F/Gas 7 and line 2 baking sheets with baking paper.

Put the courgette (zucchini) in a bowl with a good measure of oil, half the paprika or chipotle and half the cumin. Season with salt and pepper, and mix until well coated. Spread evenly in a single layer on one of the prepared baking sheets and roast for about 10 minutes. Distribute the garlic in among the courgette and continue cooking for a further 5 minutes, until the courgettes are golden in places and tender throughout.

Mix a good measure of oil in a small bowl with the remaining spices. Spread the broken tortillas on the second baking sheet, pour over the spiced oil and turn through to coat evenly. Bake in the oven for about 5–8 minutes, until toasted. Remove from the oven.

Scatter half the toasted tortillas over a large serving dish. Top with the cooked courgette and the avocado, then distribute the feta, coriander (cilantro), remaining tortillas, and the sliced chilli (if using). Serve with the wedges of lime to squeeze at the table.

Slaw

Coleslaw as we mostly know it – shredded carrot, onion and cabbage swamped with mayonnaise – is less of a salad and more of a sidekick for a sandwich or jacket potato. So slaw here, in a pedantic bid to distance itself from coleslaw, is a punchy mound of shredded vegetables with apples and pears, herbs, pomegranate and seeds, all dressed with tahini, yogurt and a bold pinch of cumin. Undoubtedly a new kitchen basic, and a distant relative to its gunky cousin.

1 small red onion, peeled and very thinly sliced

1 large lemon, halved

2 tablespoons tahini

50g (1¾oz) plain yogurt

large pinch of ground cumin

¼ small red cabbage, finely sliced

½ radicchio or 2 little gem lettuces, finely sliced

2 apples, halved, cored and thinly sliced, then cut into matchsticks (give them a squeeze of lemon to stop them browning)

2 pears, halved, cored and thinly sliced, then cut into matchsticks (give them a squeeze of lemon to stop them browning)

seeds of 1 pomegranate

small bunch of mint, leaves picked and roughly chopped

4 celery sticks, finely sliced

3 tablespoons toasted sesame seeds

3 tablespoons toasted pumpkin seeds

salt and freshly ground black pepper

Mix the red onion with a big pinch of salt and rub in, then rinse in cold water and drain well. Add a good squeeze of the lemon and put to one side.

To make the dressing, put the tahini, yogurt and another good squeeze of the lemon in a food processor or blender and blend to a smooth sauce, seasoning with a big pinch of salt and pepper. Add the cumin and stir through.

Assemble all the remaining ingredients in a large salad bowl, add the red onion and give it all a good mix to distribute. Season to taste with salt and pepper and toss with the dressing to serve.

Broccoli, Roast Onion & White Beans with Anchovy Butter

Broccoli is a favourite green vegetable. It is the likely contender for 'most frequent vegetable in the pot' when summer's bounty begins to dwindle. Cheap and versatile, broccoli likes flavour. I like my broccoli soft enough to take on flavour, no crunch necessary. Don't throw away the stalks; simply trim and peel, leaving the pale and tender inner stems to slice and cook – they're just as delicious as the 'tree-top' green florets. Anchovies and brassica are best of friends. Use purple-sprouting or Tenderstem broccoli here, if you prefer.

3 small red onions, peeled, each cut into 4 wedges

olive or vegetable oil

red wine vinegar or sherry vinegar, to taste

50g (1¾oz) unsalted butter, softened

6 anchovy fillets in oil, drained and roughly chopped

1 teaspoon finely chopped thyme or rosemary leaves

450g (1lb) small broccoli florets, or sprouting or Tenderstem broccoli

4 cloves of garlic, peeled and roughly chopped

1 x 400g (14oz) can of butter (lima) beans, drained and rinsed

salt and freshly ground black pepper

Preheat the oven to 200°C/fan 180°C/400°F/Gas 6 and line a small baking sheet with baking paper.

Put the red onion wedges on the prepared baking sheet and toss with a good measure of oil, a big pinch of salt, cracked black pepper and a splash of the vinegar. Roast for 20 minutes, until soft and charred at the edges.

Meanwhile, beat together the butter, anchovies, thyme or rosemary and a tiny splash of vinegar. Put to one side.

Put the broccoli and garlic in a pan of boiling, salted water and boil for 3–5 minutes, until tender. Drain and keep warm.

When the onions are cooked, transfer them to a large bowl. Add the butter (lima) beans, anchovy butter, and the warm broccoli, and season to taste with salt, pepper, and another splash of vinegar, if you like.

Rojak Salad of Bean Sprouts, Cucumber, Cabbage & Peanuts

Malaysian, Indonesian and Singaporean in heritage, this salad is sweet, sour, salty and spicy – intensely refreshing and packing a pungent, addictive shock of flavour. Be bold with everything and make it as bright and as beautiful as you can. Sambal oelek is an Indonesian chilli paste made with fish sauce and rice vinegar. It is readily available in bigger supermarkets and online. If you can't find any, use a good chilli sauce.

4 tablespoons tamarind pulp or sauce (see page 22, introduction)

juice of 2 limes

1 tablespoon light brown soft or palm sugar

about 1 teaspoon sambal oelek or chilli sauce, to taste

2 teaspoons fish sauce

2 tablespoons vegetable or peanut oil

1 block of extra-firm or pressed tofu, cut into bite-size pieces

1 cucumber, peeled and cut into bite-size pieces

1 green apple, peeled, cored and cut into bite-size pieces

100g (3½oz) bean sprouts

¼ small white cabbage, finely sliced

½ pineapple or firm mango, peeled, pitted, and cut into bite-size pieces

100g (3½oz) roasted peanuts, crushed

small bunch of mint or Thai basil, leaves picked and roughly chopped

salt

First, make a dressing. Whisk together the tamarind, the juice of 1½ limes, sugar, sambal oelek or chilli sauce, fish sauce and 1 tablespoon of water. Season with a little salt, to taste, remembering the fish sauce is salty. Put to one side.

Put the oil in a hot wok or frying pan, then add the tofu and fry for 8–10 minutes, until crisp and golden. Remove the tofu with a slotted spoon and dry on a plate lined with kitchen paper.

Put all the vegetables and fruit in a large salad bowl. Add the fried tofu and stir through half the peanuts and all of the dressing. Garnish with the remaining peanuts, chopped herbs, and the remaining lime, cut into wedges, then serve immediately.

Fennel, Red Onion, Olive, Orange & Pistachio Salad

Oranges come to our rescue in deepest winter – a bright jolt of colour and juicy flavour to colder-climate cooking. Served savoury in a salad, they are a transformative ingredient. This combination works flawlessly. Some chefs I have known would give very sober instructions on how to peel and segment an orange, leaving no pith or fibrous matter behind. Life is short and, once again, I don't bother. Simply peel the orange and remove any straggly pieces of pith that come away easily enough. Then, slice the orange into good-size 1cm (½in) slices. You should then be able to extract any seeds as you see them. Slices of orange framed by a thin shield of snowy pith, I think, are more beautiful than any perfectly, painstakingly segmented orange. And I should know; I have had to prep more than a few.

4 oranges, peeled and thinly sliced

1 small red onion, peeled and thinly sliced

2 tablespoons red wine vinegar

6 tablespoons olive oil

60g (2oz) kalamata or black olives, pitted

2 small fennel bulbs, tough parts trimmed and inner segments finely sliced

about 30g (1oz) pistachio nuts (or almonds or walnuts), peeled and roughly chopped

small bunch of mint, leaves picked and roughly chopped or torn

salt and freshly ground black pepper

Arrange the orange slices on a serving platter.

Put the red onion in a mixing bowl, add the vinegar and leave to macerate for about 5 minutes.

Add the olive oil, olives and sliced fennel and toss to combine. Season with salt and pepper to taste.

Spoon the onion and fennel mixture over the orange slices, then sprinkle over the pistachios (or other nuts) and scatter over the mint to serve.

Gem, Sprout & Hazelnuts with Chives & Creamy Dressing

Such an unassuming combination of ingredients for a salad, and an antidote to sprouts with their more usual, wretched, festive reputation. This green salad, with three different shades of green, is a pretty one. Choose small, freshly picked and tightly compact sprouts for optimum sweetness. The lettuce gives juicy crunch, and the chives just a whisper of allium. The hazelnuts and creamy dressing combine to make this dish sensational. Serve as a dainty, well-judged starter, or thunder-stealing big salad.

250g (9oz) Brussels sprouts, very thinly sliced or shredded

1–2 little gem lettuces, leaves separated

4 tablespoons mayonnaise

4 tablespoons crème fraîche or sour cream

small bunch of chives, chopped

juice of ½ lemon

50g (1¾oz) toasted skinned hazelnuts, coarsely chopped

salt and freshly ground black pepper

Put the sprouts and gem leaves in a large salad bowl with a big pinch of salt.

Make a dressing. Mix the mayonnaise, crème fraîche or sour cream, half the chives and the lemon juice together in a bowl, then season with salt and pepper.

Pour the dressing over the salad leaves, then top with the chopped hazelnuts and remaining chives.

Sweet Potato with Roast Corn, Black Beans & Coriander

Sweet potatoes are best combined with bold flavours and an assortment of textures as a foil to their sweet, fudgy character when cooked. A root vegetable and completely unrelated to white potatoes, sweet potatoes are rich in fibre, vitamins and minerals. Combined with roast corn and beans they pack more flavour than you might have thought possible. Slash the top of the cooked sweet potato, shovelling in some of the filling and letting some spill lavishly out onto the plate.

4 small–medium sweet potatoes

60g (2¼oz) unsalted butter

3 cloves of garlic, peeled and crushed

2 teaspoons ground cumin

½–1 teaspoon chilli flakes, or more to taste

4 corns on the cob

1 large red onion, peeled and cut into quarters

1 bunch of spring onions (scallions), thinly sliced

2 teaspoons runny honey

zest and juice of 1 unwaxed lime

small bunch of coriander (cilantro), roughly chopped

2 tablespoons peanut or olive oil

1 x 400g (14oz) can of black or kidney beans, drained and rinsed

smoked paprika, for dusting

salt and freshly ground black pepper

TO SERVE
chilli sauce (choose your favourite)

sour cream

Preheat the oven to 200°C/fan 180°C/400°F/Gas 6.

Pierce holes in the sweet potatoes with a skewer, then bake them for about 30–40 minutes, until cooked through. Remove from the oven and keep warm.

While the potatoes are cooking, make a spiced butter. Mash the butter, garlic, cumin and chilli together in a small bowl, and season with salt and pepper, to taste. Put to one side.

Cut 4 pieces of foil large enough to hold a cob and and some wedges of onion. Place a cob on each piece, divide the onion equally between each cob parcel and slather each cob with spiced butter. Divide the spring onions (scallions) between each, and bring up the edges of the foil to seal as individual parcels. Bake for 30–35 minutes, until the corn is tender.

Make a dressing with the honey, lime zest and juice, coriander (cilantro) and oil, and season with salt and pepper to taste. Put to one side.

Once the corn is cooked, drain the cooking juices into a mixing bowl and shuck the corn kernels into the bowl. Stir in the beans and check the seasoning. Keep warm.

Slice the cooked sweet potatoes through the top and stuff each with the corn and bean mixture, dust with paprika and pop the potatoes back in the oven for about 3 minutes to warm through.

Remove from the oven and spoon the dressing in and over each sweet potato. Serve with chilli sauce and sour cream at the table.

Mattar Paneer

This is an easy curry to make using unfailingly useful frozen peas. Serve with warm naan or chapati to scoop and mop, or in combination with other curries and Indian dishes. Softly spiced, the peas are cooked here with ginger and tomatoes, made luscious and rich with cream and bolstered yet more with chopped coriander (cilantro) and lemon. I would happily make twice this quantity and reheat the leftovers the next day – the flavour will only get better given time. Some jarred Indian pickles and chutneys would also be welcome alongside.

sunflower oil

400g (14oz) paneer, cut in to bite-size pieces (cooked potatoes also work well in place of the paneer)

2 teaspoons cumin seeds

2 tablespoons finely grated (shredded) root ginger

4 cloves of garlic, peeled and finely chopped

½–1 teaspoon medium–hot chilli powder

2 teaspoons turmeric

2 teaspoons ground coriander

300g (10½oz) tomatoes, finely chopped

200g (7oz) frozen peas, defrosted

100ml (3½fl oz) double (heavy) cream or plain yogurt

handful of coriander (cilantro), finely chopped

lemon wedges

salt and freshly ground black pepper

Put enough oil in a large non-stick frying pan to coat the base, and place over a moderate to high heat. Add the paneer and fry until it begins to turn golden brown, about 2–3 minutes. Using a slotted spoon, remove the paneer from the oil and leave to drain and rest on kitchen paper.

Add another measure of oil to the pan and cook the cumin seeds until they begin to crackle and pop, then add the ginger and garlic and cook for 30 seconds, until fragrant.

Add the ground spices and stir well, then add the chopped tomatoes and allow to cook for about 5 minutes, until thick. Add the fried paneer and the peas, along with 200ml (7fl oz) of water. Check the seasoning, adding salt and pepper to taste.

Bring to a boil, then reduce the heat to moderate and simmer partially covered for about 10 minutes, stirring occasionally. Stir in the cream or yogurt and remove from the heat. Leave to rest, covered, for at least 10 minutes to allow the flavours to develop.

Serve sprinkled with coriander (cilantro) and with a lemon wedge for squeezing.

Apricot, Cauliflower & Pine Nut Tabbouleh

Tabbouleh gets bad press. This recipe should help put the record straight. I tested it on a friend who hates tabbouleh – and now doesn't. You must have more green in your tabbouleh than any other colour. This unwritten cookery lore ultimately helps to banish thoughts of those dreary beige tumbles, omnipresent as the salad option in cafés and sandwich outlets. Make it green, super-green. You should be searching through a sea of green for the bulgur wheat.

150g (5½oz) coarse bulgur wheat or wholewheat Israeli couscous

warm water, to cover

1 small cauliflower (about 650g/ 1lb 7oz), quartered

zest and juice of 1 unwaxed lemon

50ml (1¾fl oz) olive oil

2 tablespoons pomegranate molasses (or use extra lemon juice and brown sugar, to taste)

½ teaspoon ground cinnamon

½–1 clove of garlic, peeled and crushed

150g (5½oz) dried apricots, finely chopped

50g (1¾oz) pine nuts, or cashews, walnuts or almonds, toasted

very large bunch of flat-leaf parsley, leaves picked and finely chopped

large bunch of mint, leaves picked and finely chopped

2 teaspoons sumac

½–1 teaspoon chilli flakes (optional)

salt and freshly ground black pepper

Put the bulgur wheat in a mixing bowl and cover with warm water by about 10cm (4in). Soak for 10 minutes, then drain well. Meanwhile, put the cauliflower in a food processor and pulse into small pieces. Put to one side.

Make the dressing. Put the lemon zest and juice in a mixing bowl, add the olive oil, pomegranate molasses, cinnamon and crushed garlic. Mix well and put to one side.

Put the cauliflower pieces into a large serving bowl along with the drained bulgur, apricots, pine nuts, herbs, sumac and chilli flakes, if using. Pour the dressing over the salad and mix well. Check the seasoning, to taste.

You can serve immediately or, if you'd rather, leave the tabbouleh for about 30 minutes for the flavours to mingle and the grain to absorb the dressing.

Green Salad for Now

If you're going to eat salad for lunch, I say let it be a great, big, gorgeous gallimaufry. This salad is a long way from limp lettuce, cucumber that has seen better days and a few rock-hard tomato wedges. It's a triumphant assembly of the colour green and gives new definition to green salad. Use any green vegetable, salad or fruits you like, summon up your inner flower-arranging skills (here's my attempt, super-pretty, reassuringly human), jumble together with the dressing, and then eat it.

200g (7oz) Tenderstem or purple sprouting broccoli or small broccoli florets

150g (5½oz) green beans, trimmed

150g (5½oz) frozen shelled edamame

150g (5½oz) frozen or fresh peas

3 tablespoons olive oil

1 clove of garlic, peeled and finely chopped

150g (5½oz) crème fraîche, sour cream or Greek yogurt

small bunch of basil, leaves picked

small bunch of mint, leaves picked

3 sprigs of tarragon, leaves picked

juice of 1 lemon

150g (5½oz) baby spinach leaves or lamb's lettuce

1 large apple, finely sliced

½ fennel bulb, trimmed and inner part finely sliced

2 avocados, flesh cut into bite-size pieces

1 small lettuce, such as little gem, leaves separated

salt and freshly ground black pepper

Bring a large pan of salted water to a boil and have a bowl of iced or very cold water ready to refresh the vegetables.

Cook the broccoli, beans, edamame and peas, in separate batches, for about 2 minutes each, until just tender. As each vegetable batch cooks, remove it from the water using a slotted spoon and transfer it to the cold water to chill, before draining well.

Blend together the olive oil, garlic and crème fraîche (or alternative) in a bowl, and season with salt and pepper to taste. Add half the herbs and all the lemon juice and blend again to a smooth dressing.

Assemble the drained vegetables with the remaining herbs, and the spinach leaves or lamb's lettuce, apple, fennel, avocado and lettuce leaves. Season with salt and pepper to taste, then dress to serve.

Jalfrezi Peppers with Chickpeas & Coriander

I'm never all that keen on raw (bell) peppers, but cooked ones take some beating. Fried or grilled (broiled), the flesh collapses, turning luscious and slippery soft, a beautiful canvas for flavour. Jalfrezi means 'hot fry'. First, you blend half the ingredients to make a sauce, you then fry the rest. It is a failsafe curry preparation. You could add strips of chicken, pork or beef to cook (or use leftover roast meat) with the onions and peppers, but I rarely bother.

2 onions, peeled and cut into 0.5cm (¼in) slices

3 cloves of garlic, peeled and finely sliced

2 tablespoons grated (shredded) root ginger

½–1 teaspoon chilli flakes, or powder (mild or hot, as you like)

juice of 1 lemon

½ teaspoon salt, plus extra to season

2 tablespoons vegetable oil

2 teaspoons cumin seeds

2 teaspoons mustard seeds

2–4 (bell) peppers (any colour), depending on size, deseeded and cut into 1.5cm (⅝in) slices

2 ripe tomatoes, roughly chopped

1 x 400g (14oz) can of chickpeas (garbanzos), drained and rinsed

2 teaspoons garam masala

freshly ground black pepper

TO SERVE
1–2 green chillies, sliced (optional; remove the seeds to reduce heat, if you like)

handful or coriander (cilantro) leaves, chopped

seasoned yogurt (see page 54)

Put half the onion, along with the garlic, the ginger and the chilli flakes or powder into a blender or mini food processor with half the lemon juice, the ½ teaspoon of salt and 50ml (1¾fl oz) of water. Blitz to a purée.

Heat the oil in a large frying pan or wok over a moderate to high heat, and add the cumin seeds and mustard seeds. Fry for 2–3 minutes, until they begin to crackle and pop. Add the onion purée and cook for 5 minutes, until it begins to stick and smell fragrant.

Add the remaining sliced onion and the (bell) peppers. Reduce the heat to moderate and cook, covered, for 15 minutes, until the onion and peppers have softened and are beginning to caramelize.

Add the tomatoes and chickpeas (garbanzos) and cook for 2 minutes more, then check the dish for seasoning, adjusting with more salt and some pepper if you like. Add the garam masala and mix well.

Add the rest of the lemon juice and sprinkle over the chopped chillies (if using) and coriander (cilantro).

Serve with the seasoned yogurt, and plain rice or Indian flatbreads and jarred Indian chutney and/or pickles.

Green Beans with Tomato, Turmeric & Spiced Butter

When green and runner (string) beans come into season, they tend to come as an avalanche, piled high and cheap. And when you tire of those first batches simply boiled or steamed and dressed with a little butter or olive oil, make this recipe: a soft tangle of green beans, slow-cooked with tomatoes and spiced butter. It is a heady assembly and good with roast meat or fish, or as a standalone with flatbreads to scoop. Best served warm, never piping hot.

50g (1¾oz) butter

1 teaspoon ground turmeric

1 tablespoon coriander seeds, toasted and lightly crushed

3 cloves of garlic, peeled and finely chopped

olive oil

1 small onion, peeled and finely chopped

1 x 400g (14oz) can of whole plum tomatoes

1 cinnamon stick

400g (14oz) green beans, trimmed, or runner (string) beans, trimmed and cut into 3

large pinch of chilli flakes, plus extra (optional) to taste

about 200ml (7fl oz) boiling water

100g (3½oz) seasoned yogurt (see page 54)

small bunch of dill or flat-leaf parsley, roughly chopped

salt and freshly ground black pepper

Heat the butter in a small frying pan over a moderate to high heat with the turmeric, half the coriander seeds and half the garlic until the butter just begins to bubble. Remove from the heat and allow to infuse.

Put enough oil in a medium pan to coat the base, and place over a moderate heat. Add the onion and cook for about 8–10 minutes, until soft. Strain over half the spiced butter and add the remaining garlic into the pan. Cook for about 30 seconds, then add the tomatoes and cinnamon. Season to taste with salt and pepper. Cook for 10–15 minutes, until thickened and rich-tasting.

Add the green or runner (string) beans, chilli flakes and boiling water. Cover the pan, turn the heat down as low as possible and cook until the beans have softened to your liking – about 30 minutes (you may need to add more water from time to time if the pan dries out too much). You want the beans soft, not crunchy, collapsing in among the tomato sauce.

When the beans are cooked, check the seasoning, adding salt, pepper or more chilli flakes to your liking. Remove the cinnamon stick, add the seasoned yogurt and top with the dill or parsley and remaining coriander seeds. Strain over the remaining spiced butter.

CHEESE

'Rat-trap' was the name my dad gave the chunk of cheese in the fridge. The cheese (for mostly there was just the one sort) was a creamy hue, somewhere between butterscotch yellow and apricot orange, and waxy to the touch. The cheese in the fridge didn't seem ever to diminish or grow in size; it was always the same, about a quarter gone from a full block. I know this because, as a child, I would crudely slice hunks of cheese from the packet directly on the fridge shelf and pop them into my mouth, with the refrigerator door as ludicrous protection, freezer door beneath still shut, and legs clearly visible to anyone passing. Despite this covert cheese eating, the next day, and the day after that, there was always yet more cheese in the fridge; this seemed to me to be especially bewitching, a never-ending cheese of sorts. Of course, the cheese was replenished, and what I never really noticed was that its rate of replenishment was simply down to the rate at which it was eaten. Its mobility in and out of the fridge was testament to how indispensable it was to the food my mum cooked and made for us all at the time. From new in the packet to total demolition, in no time at all, it was a dietary stalwart – and unthinkable was the fridge that lacked it.

This was Cheddar, the cheese of my childhood, and while other cheeses did make guest appearances (Brie and Stilton spring to mind), mostly it was workhorse Cheddar. In it went, to pretty much everything from sandwiches to quiches to scones, as a canapé or children's party fodder with cubes of pineapple (who can resist?), or generously grated to top my mum's herculean fish pie. It was also the only cheese we ever grated to serve with pasta (Parmesan came much later) and the table would often be set with both cheese and grater, ready for repeated action. Cheddar cheese, as we consumed it, was a functional ingredient, intrinsic to the weekly shop – which is why, I suppose, the name 'rat-trap' stuck in our household at the time.

Now with my own fridge to furnish with cheese, yogurt, milk and more, Cheddar remains a bedrock of the weekly shop (though perhaps not used with quite the same intensity as in the

1980s), although other cheeses do find preference. I love cheese and, as ingredients go, I can think of no other that affords the same flexibility of use and also knack to sate the appetite as a standalone morsel. Without fail, I will always have in my fridge a relatively hard cheese of sorts – this type of cheese is privy to the same swift fridge raid of my youth, eaten as is, sharp complex flavours bursting and biting down on the tongue. In addition, there will also be either Parmesan or pecorino, salty and crystalline to nibble or grate as the crucial finishing flurry to so many pasta dishes, soups and risottos. Feta or halloumi also feature commonly, as the easy, salty boost to many different recipes. There might also be the luxury of a soft, possibly more expensive, cheese to scoop or spoon like butter, ripe and yielding and inescapably delicious, as these sorts of cheeses tend to be.

I've broken this chapter down into broadly three sections: Cheddar (and ancestors thereof), blue and soft cheese, and feta and goat cheese, with each grouping of cheese presenting different applications, some cooked and some not. Heat transforms some cheeses in a mind-bendingly good way, with the cheese changing in characteristic, melting obediently. Given a fierce heat, baked alongside potatoes or numerous combinations of vegetables, or grilled (broiled) between slices of good bread, cheese is compellingly unctuous. In dishes where the cheese hasn't been cooked, but rather strewn over the finished dish, cheese can serve to contrast and flatter. I can think of few things more inviting to eat than a creamy, oozing gorgonzola, barely able to hold its form, spooned onto something blistering and hot – polenta, for example, with the heat beneath jump-starting the cheese, bidding it to run free. More on this later (see page 134).

Cheese is a primal and also deeply sophisticated food, capable of sparking supreme alchemy in the kitchen. Certain cheeses can lend gravitas to thrifty, everyday ingredients, while others can represent the utmost luxury to anticipate and savour. Take the Enchilada Mushrooms on page 133: why is the recipe here in the cheese chapter of **New Kitchen Basics**?

Because, for me, the wisdom of popular Mexican dishes, such as taco and enchilada, is the balance fostered between using the thrifty staples of corn and beans with more expensive ingredients, such as cheese and meat. Less is more – it's endlessly clever cooking. In that recipe you can use mature aged Cheddar in lieu of more traditional queso añejo, and I rather like the manner in which the cheese melts, like magma.

If, for some reason, you aren't able to get hold of Cheddar, then Gruyère, Emmental, Gouda, Cantal or Tomme are all good alternatives.

The variation and very regionality of cheese make it a colossal topic. I've given just 12 cheese recipes in this chapter, presenting, I hope, new approaches to some of the most popular cheeses in retail. In **New Kitchen Basics**, when it comes to cheese, there are no hard-and-fast rules. Leave no cheese unturned.

Cauliflower Cheese Cakes

Three-cheese Dauphinoise

Grilled Cheddar & Jalapeño Popper Sandwich

Glamorgan Sausage

Enchilada Mushrooms

Gorgonzola with Polenta, Walnuts & Radicchio

Stilton & Fig Wholemeal Scones

Mozzarella with Roast Stone Fruit

Fried Halloumi with Aubergine & Butter Beans

Roast Onions with Sherry Vinegar,
Thyme & Goat Cheese

Whipped Feta with Blitzed Carrots
& Roast Chickpeas

Leek, Artichoke & Feta Filo Pie

Cauliflower Cheese Cakes

Cauliflower cheese in diminutive cake form, this recipe is a doddle to assemble and might give cauliflower baked with béchamel some respite in your repertoire. Blitzed raw, the cauliflower is bound with cheese, egg, mustard – and more – to bake in the prepared muffin tins. These are perfect served warm with extra Dijon mustard on the table to swoop through; any leftovers might make for a welcome lunchbox addition.

½ cauliflower head with stalk removed (about 250g/9oz)

200g (7oz) Cheddar or Emmental, coarsely grated (shredded)

2 eggs, lightly beaten

¼ nutmeg, grated, or more to taste

50g (1¾oz) dried breadcrumbs

2 tablespoons Dijon mustard

1 tablespoon picked thyme leaves

½ teaspoon salt

½ teaspoon freshly ground black pepper

unsalted butter, for greasing

MAKES 12

Preheat the oven to 200°C/fan 180°C/400°F/Gas 6.

Blitz the cauliflower in a food processor (work in batches) into very small pieces about the size of peas. Alternatively, use a large knife to break down the cauliflower, chopping it well.

In a bowl, mix the cauliflower with the cheese, eggs, nutmeg, breadcrumbs, mustard, thyme, salt and pepper.

Lightly grease a 12-hole muffin tin with butter and spoon around 1½ tablespoons of the mixture into each hole.

Put the tin into the oven and cook for about 15 minutes, until the cakes are golden brown and bubbling at the edges. Leave to cool in the tin for 5 minutes before removing – you might need to run a spatula or spoon around the edges to gently nudge them out.

Three-cheese Dauphinoise

I have cooked more potatoes dauphinoise in restaurant kitchens than I care to count. This method does away with cooking the thinly sliced raw potatoes from the off in the baking dish (hours and hours…!). Here, with more consistent results and a considerably quicker cooking time, the sliced potatoes are par-cooked on the hob in the cream and then finished off in the oven. The three different cheeses give depth and a sense of decadence: nutty Gruyère lays the foundations, Parmesan imbues the cream with a complex fruity flavour and valiant Cheddar melts, bronzing, as the potatoes finish in the oven.

250ml (9fl oz) double (heavy) cream

150ml (5fl oz) whole milk

2 cloves of garlic, peeled and crushed

1 teaspoon thyme leaves

1 bay leaf

¼ nutmeg, grated, or more to taste

800g (1lb 12oz) waxy potatoes, peeled and very thinly sliced

1 teaspoon salt

50g (1¾oz) Gruyère or other mild, firm cheese, grated (shredded)

30g (1oz) Parmesan, finely grated (shredded)

50g (1¾oz) Cheddar or other sharp, strong cheese, coarsely grated (shredded)

freshly ground black pepper

Bring the cream and milk to the boil in a large pan over a high heat with the garlic, thyme, bay and nutmeg, and a seasoning of black pepper. Add the potatoes and salt, reduce the heat and simmer gently for about 10 minutes, until the potatoes are just about cooked through. Use a sharp knife to test – you want the potatoes tender, but not soft or broken down.

Meanwhile preheat the oven to 180°C/fan160°C/350°F/Gas 4.

Spread the Gruyère over the base of a baking dish large enough to house the potatoes.

Remove the bay leaf from the potato mixture and add the Parmesan. Gently tip the mixture into the dish and spread evenly. Cover loosely with foil (try not to let the foil touch the top of the mixture) and bake for 35 minutes.

Then remove the foil, sprinkle the Cheddar on top and bake for a further 10 minutes, until nicely browned. Remove from the oven and allow to rest for at least 5 minutes before serving.

Grilled Cheddar & Jalapeño Popper Sandwich

I like the name 'popper' – a grilled (broiled) cheese sandwich by any other name. Cream cheese can be bland and fairly ordinary. Here it gets turbo-charged with tangy Cheddar, fiery jalapeño chilli and a musky pinch of cumin. Add bacon? When it comes to grilled cheese sandwiches, aim for the stars…

200g (7oz) full-fat cream cheese

1–2 jalapeño or green chillies, finely chopped (remove the seeds to reduce heat, if you like)

½ teaspoon ground cumin

1 clove of garlic, peeled and crushed

40g (1½oz) unsalted butter, softened

8 slices of white bread (choose a sturdy bread that toasts well)

300g (10½oz) Cheddar, coarsely grated (shredded)

8 slices of cooked streaky bacon (optional)

freshly ground black pepper

MAKES 4 POPPERS

In a bowl, mix together the cream cheese, jalapeño or green chillies, cumin and garlic, then season with pepper.

Butter one side of each slice of bread. Turn over 4 of the slices and spread each of these with equal amounts of the cream-cheese mixture. Top with the cheese and the bacon, if using. Top with the remaining bread slices, with the buttered sides facing outwards.

Place a large frying pan over a moderate to high heat. Fry the sandwiches (you might need to do this batches) for about 4 minutes on each side, until golden brown with the cheese melted through the middle.

Remove from the heat and serve immediately – with plenty of paper napkins!

Glamorgan Sausage

The Glamorgan sausage has remarkable Welsh ancestry, with recipes dating as far back as the 12th century and coming right through to that modern-day bastion of good, sensible cooking practice: the Women's Institute. Leek and cheese cloaked in breadcrumbs is a humble, triumphant (round of applause) combination. Fried first and then finished off in the oven, these Glamorgan sausages reign as a new kitchen basic of greedy proportion. Make some.

30g (1oz) unsalted butter

2 leeks, trimmed and finely chopped

220g (7¾oz) fresh breadcrumbs

2 teaspoons thyme leaves

2 teaspoons English mustard

220g (7¾oz) Caerphilly, Lancashire or mild Cheddar, coarsely grated (shredded)

3 eggs

40ml (1¼fl oz) whole milk or single (light) cream

¼ nutmeg, grated, or more to taste

60g (2¼oz) plain (all-purpose) flour

vegetable or sunflower oil

salt and freshly ground black pepper

MAKES 8 SAUSAGES

Melt the butter in a large saucepan over a moderate heat. Add the leeks with a good pinch of salt and cook for about 10 minutes, until soft. Remove from the heat and leave to cool.

Once the leeks are cool, put 120g (4¼oz) of the breadcrumbs in a large bowl with the thyme, mustard, cheese, 2 of the eggs, the milk or cream and the cooked leeks. Add the nutmeg to taste and season with salt and pepper. Chill the mixture for at least 10 minutes to rest and firm up.

Using your hands, form the chilled mixture into 8 sausage shapes and chill for about a further 20 minutes, to firm up again.

Preheat the oven to 180°C/fan 160°C/350°F/Gas 4.

Lightly beat the remaining egg and put it in a bowl large enough to fit a sausage. Take another 2 bowls and put the flour in one and the remaining breadcrumbs in the other. Coat the sausages by dredging first in the flour, then dipping in the egg and then coating in the breadcrumbs.

Put enough oil in a non-stick frying pan to coat the base, and place over a moderate to high heat. Add the sausages and fry for about 2–3 minutes in total, turning until golden on all sides. Transfer to a baking sheet to finish cooking in the oven for about 15 minutes, until piping hot through. Remove from the oven and serve immediately.

Enchilada Mushrooms

Soft tortillas wrapped snugly round mushrooms and black beans with cumin, chilli and oregano: less of a recipe, more of a standard for you to then riff on. Why not make this version first, then experiment with other combinations – corn, shredded cooked meat or poultry, chorizo, courgettes (zucchini), chipotle, ancho or jalapeño chilli, flaked cooked fish... and more?

vegetable or sunflower oil

1 large onion, peeled and finely diced

2 cloves of garlic, peeled and crushed

1–2 teaspoons chilli flakes or hot paprika; or use chipotle chilli flakes, to taste

1 tablespoon ground cumin

1 teaspoon dried oregano

½ teaspoon salt, plus extra to season

1 x 400g (14oz) can of whole plum tomatoes, blended in a bowl or jug until smooth

250g (9oz) field or button mushrooms, sliced into 1cm (½in) slices

2 green chillies, finely chopped (remove the seeds to reduce heat, if you like)

1 x 400g (14oz) can of kidney or black beans, drained and rinsed

100g (3½oz) sour cream, plus extra to serve

150g (5½oz) aged, strong Cheddar, coarsely grated (shredded)

8 medium wheat or soft corn tortillas

freshly ground black pepper

small bunch of coriander (cilantro), leaves picked and roughly chopped (finely chop some of the stalks, too, if you like, and fry with the mushrooms)

Put enough oil in medium pan to coat the base, and place over a moderate heat. Add half the onion and fry for about 8–10 minutes, or until soft. Add the half the garlic, half the chilli, half the cumin, half the oregano, and the half teaspoon of salt and cook for 30 seconds, until fragrant. Add the tomatoes and 200ml (7fl oz) of water, and cook, uncovered, for 10 minutes, until thick and rich. Check the seasoning, remove from the heat and put to one side.

Preheat the oven to 190°C/fan 170°C/325°F/Gas 5. Grease an oven dish measuring about 20 x 30cm (8 x 12in).

Heat a splash of oil in a fresh pan over a moderate heat. Add the remaining onion and fry for about 8–10 minutes, until soft. Add the sliced mushrooms and the remaining garlic (and the coriander/cilantro stalks, if using) and cook for about 3 minutes, until the mushrooms release their liquid. Continue to cook until the liquid has evaporated.

Add the remaining chilli, cumin and oregano, along with the chopped green chilli and the beans. Season to taste with salt and pepper. Stir through half the sour cream and 100g (3½oz) of the cheese.

Divide the mushroom mixture between the 8 tortillas, placing the filling just off-centre and ensuring each tortilla is filled, rolled and placed seam-side down in the greased baking dish. Pour the tomato sauce over the top and sprinkle with the last of the cheese.

Bake in the oven for about 20 minutes, until bubbling and lightly browned. Then remove from the oven and rest for about 5 minutes. Serve topped with additional sour cream and the coriander.

Gorgonzola with Polenta, Walnuts & Radicchio

One autumn a few years ago, I visited a friend studying in Bologna, a town in Emilia-Romagna, northern Italy. We drove in a tiny car, holding too many people, to an unremarkable-looking restaurant in the hills. There we had many glasses of wine and this plate of food. An unforgettable dish, using the simplest of ingredients, it is an excellent way to show off this most irrepressible of cheeses. The gorgonzola melts helplessly onto the polenta, with the radicchio and walnuts giving crunch and captivating bitterness.

50g (1¾oz) unsalted butter, diced, plus extra for greasing and topping

900ml (31fl oz) whole milk and water at a 50:50 ratio

2 cloves of garlic, peeled and thinly sliced

1 tablespoon thyme leaves

½ teaspoon salt, plus extra for seasoning

150g (5½oz) coarse polenta

50g (13½oz) Parmesan, grated (shredded)

1 small radicchio, sliced into thick ribbons

olive oil, for frying

good pinch of sugar

about ½ teaspoon red wine vinegar or balsamic vinegar

150g (5½oz) gorgonzola or other mild, soft, blue cheese, roughly chopped or broken up

big handful of hazelnuts, walnuts or almonds, lightly toasted and roughly chopped

small bunch of flat-leaf parsley, leaves picked and roughly chopped

freshly ground black pepper

Grease a baking dish measuring about 20 x 30cm (8 x 12in) with a little butter.

Put the milk/water, garlic and half the thyme in a deep saucepan with the salt and bring to a simmer over a moderate–high heat. Pour the polenta into the pan in a steady, thin stream, whisking all the time to ensure there are no lumps. Once the mixture gets too thick to work with a whisk, change to a wooden spoon.

Bring the polenta mixture back to a simmer over a medium heat, and continue to cook, stirring constantly, for about 5 minutes. Turn down the heat to low and continue to cook gently for about 40 minutes, until very thick and the polenta has cooked out. Give the mixture a vigorous stir every couple of minutes to stop the base sticking too much (and stick it will). Remove from the heat. Stir in the Parmesan and diced butter and pour the mixture into the greased baking dish. Preheat the oven to 190°C/fan 170°C/375°F/Gas 5.

Top the polenta with a few extra knobs of butter and bake in the hot oven for about 15 minutes, until beginning to brown.

Meanwhile, in a large frying pan over a moderate heat, fry the radicchio in a splash of olive oil with the remaining thyme, the sugar and a good pinch of salt, until wilted and beginning to brown. Add the vinegar at the very end and remove from the heat.

When the polenta is ready, top with the gorgonzola and return to the oven for 5 more minutes, until the cheese is melted. Remove from the oven and top with the radicchio, then scatter over the nuts and the parsley.

Stilton & Fig Wholemeal Scones

There's something to be said for bringing just a few simple ingredients together swiftly in a bowl, and for the outcome when baked to taste as good as this. I've loved making scones, a kitchen basic, ever since I first started cooking: plain to start with, then gradually introducing different ingredients and switching flours. I've used wholemeal (wholewheat) flour here for its nutty character, which I think flatters the Stilton and the fig. It is crucial to let the scones sit and rest on a wire rack for 10 minutes on exit from the oven, to allow the steam to dissipate and the scone crumb to firm up.

225g (8oz) wholemeal (wholewheat) flour

225g (8oz) self-raising flour, plus extra for dusting

110g (3¾oz) cold unsalted butter, cut into small dice

150g (5½oz) Stilton, or any firm blue cheese, crumbled

6 large dried figs or apricots, or dates, roughly chopped

1 teaspoon salt

1 teaspoon coarsely cracked black pepper

1 egg

150ml (5½fl oz) whole milk

MAKES ABOUT 8 SCONES

Preheat the oven to 180°C/fan 160°C/350°F/Gas 4. Line a baking sheet with baking paper.

Place the flours and butter in a mixing bowl and rub together with your fingertips until the mixture resembles fine breadcrumbs (pulsing in a food processor is a good way to do this quickly).

Add the Stilton, figs, salt and pepper, and mix well.

Beat the egg and the milk together in a jug. Gradually add all but 1 tablespoon of the egg and milk mixture to the dry ingredients in the bowl, and use a metal spoon to gently bring together to form a cohesive dough. Work quickly and with as little mixing as possible.

Tip the dough out onto a floured surface – it won't be completely smooth and will have a few fissures – and gently pat out to about 3cm (1¼in) thick.

Using a metal cutter, stamp out as many 7cm (2¾in) rounds as you can and place on the lined sheet, then gently pull together the remaining dough, pat it out again and cut more rounds until you've used up all the dough. It will do no harm if the last few rounds are a bit misshapen, to prevent any over-working of the dough.

Brush the top of each scone with the remaining tablespoon of egg-and-milk mixture and place the sheet in the oven to bake for 16–20 minutes, or until risen and golden.

Remove from the oven and cool on a wire rack for at least 10 minutes.

Mozzarella with Roast Stone Fruit

If cheese served with fruit is an obvious combination, mozzarella with roast peaches is the stand-out – new kitchen basic – option. Buy best-quality mozzarella (buffalo is ideal, or use burrata) to accompany the fruit. My favourite fruit for this is peaches, but any ripe stone fruit will work. Roasted, the fruit turns sweet and extra-luscious, with the creamy, lactic mozzarella offering up superb balance. The torn and toasted ciabatta gives good bulk to this sultry, summery recipe, but omit the bread if you prefer.

4 ripe peaches, nectarines, red plums or apricots, halved and stoned, or about 400g (14oz) stoned cherries

2 tablespoons red wine vinegar

1 tablespoon runny honey or caster (superfine) sugar

½ loaf of ciabatta or similar-style bread, crusts removed and torn into small pieces

2 tablespoons olive oil, plus extra for toasting

pinch of chilli flakes (optional)

250g (9oz) buffalo mozzarella, roughly torn into 8 pieces

small bunch of basil, leaves picked and roughly torn if large

salt and freshly ground black pepper

Preheat the oven to 220°C/fan 200°C/425°F/Gas 7. Line a baking dish with baking paper.

Arrange the fruit cut-side up in the lined baking dish and sprinkle with 1 tablespoon of the vinegar, along with the honey or sugar. Roast for about 15–20 minutes, or until the tops of the fruit begin to bubble and char at the edges, and syrupy juices form in the bottom of the baking dish. Remove from the oven and leave to cool slightly.

Meanwhile, in a separate baking dish, mix the bread with a good measure of olive oil and a good pinch of salt. Bake for about 8–10 minutes in the hot oven, until the bread is nicely toasted.

In a small bowl, mix together the 2 tablespoons of olive oil and the remaining vinegar, along with any juices left over from roasting the fruit, and the chilli flakes, if using. Season with salt and pepper.

On a large serving dish, arrange the peaches (or other fruit) and toasted bread and pour over the dressing. Add the mozzarella and basil. Drizzle with a little more olive oil and serve.

Fried Halloumi with Aubergine & Butter Beans

Halloumi is often the default cheesy slab to fry or grill (broil). Served as a meaty substitute at a barbecue, like it so often is, this cheese can lack any real interest, save its characteristic squeaky saltiness. Halloumi can also tend to dry out when cooked. As a result, I think it is essential to serve halloumi alongside something full-tasting and unctuous; something that has a bit of moisture to it. Tomatoes and aubergine (eggplant), cooked with honey and paprika, make this dish just the ticket. Serve with pita or flatbreads to mop.

4 tablespoons olive oil, plus extra to finish and serve

4 cloves of garlic, peeled and finely chopped

1 x 400g (14oz) can of whole plum tomatoes or 400g (14oz) fresh tomatoes

2 teaspoons ground cumin

2 teaspoons sweet paprika (not smoked)

½ teaspoon chilli flakes

1 teaspoon salt, plus extra to season

1 tablespoon runny honey

2 large aubergines (eggplants), peeled and finely diced

2 x 400g (14oz) cans of butter (lima) beans, drained and rinsed

zest and juice of ½ unwaxed lemon

small bunch of flat-leaf parsley, leaves picked and finely chopped, plus extra to serve

450g (1lb) halloumi, cut into 1cm (½in) slices

pita or flatbreads, to serve

freshly ground black pepper

Put 3 tablespoons of the olive oil in a pan over a moderate heat. Add the garlic and fry for about 30 seconds, then add the tomatoes, spices, salt and honey and cook for 2 minutes, until starting to thicken.

Add the aubergine (eggplant) and 200ml (7fl oz) of water and cover with a lid. Reduce the heat slightly to bring the liquid to a simmer for about 20 minutes, stirring occasionally, until the sauce is lovely and thick and the aubergine is soft and cooked through. Add a splash of water if it dries out before the aubergine is cooked. Check the seasoning and adjust with salt and pepper as necessary.

Stir through the butter (lima) beans and cook for 2 minutes more for the flavours to mingle. Remove from the heat and add the lemon zest and juice and the parsley. Mix together, then put to one side to keep warm.

Put the remaining oil in a non-stick frying pan over a moderate heat. Add the halloumi and cook each side for about 1–2 minutes, until golden and crisp.

To serve, add the aubergine and butter beans to a wide, flat serving dish and top with the fried halloumi. Sprinkle with parsley and serve with warm pita breads.

Roast Onions with Sherry Vinegar, Thyme & Goat Cheese

The goat cheese should steal the show here, but, if I'm honest, I think it's probably the onions that get the gold medal. Roasting half the onions whole to then squash out the soft flesh and whizz into a dressing with thyme and vinegar, and roasting the other half in quarters until they are at soft collapse, gives a mind-blowing and elegant depth to the dish. Soft goat cheese, with its tart, earthy flavour, pairs beautifully with the sweetly combusted onions. Serve as a first course or light lunch to really wow your guests.

1kg (2lb 4oz) small red onions or banana shallots, half of them peeled and left whole, half peeled and quartered

3 tablespoons olive or vegetable oil

3 tablespoons sherry vinegar or balsamic vinegar

1 teaspoon thyme leaves

150g (5½oz) mixed leaves, such as a combination of watercress, rocket (arugula) and baby spinach

200g (7oz) soft goat cheese, crumbled or sliced into smaller pieces

20g (¾oz) toasted pumpkin or sunflower seeds, or walnuts

salt and freshly ground black pepper

Preheat the oven to 200°C/fan 180°C/400°F/Gas 6. Line 2 baking sheets with baking paper.

Put the whole peeled red onions or shallots on one of the lined baking sheets and roast for about 40 minutes, until the flesh is completely soft and pulpy. Remove from the oven and allow to cool.

While the whole onions are cooking, put the red onion or shallot wedges on the other lined baking sheet and toss with 1 tablespoon of the oil, 1 tablespoon of the vinegar and a good pinch of salt and freshly ground black pepper. Roast for 20 minutes, until beginning to soften and char at the edges. Remove from the oven and allow to cool.

Once both sets of onion are cool, make a roasted onion dressing. Cut off the ends of the whole onions and squeeze the flesh from the skins. Discard the skins, finely chop the soft flesh and put in a mixing bowl. Add the remaining 2 tablespoons of vinegar and 2 tablespoons of oil and the thyme leaves, mix well and season to taste with salt and pepper.

Separate the layers of the cooked onion wedges and put to one side. Put the mixed leaves in a large salad bowl, pour over the roast onion dressing and toss to coat. Check the seasoning.

Add the onion layers and the cheese to the dressed leaves. Top with the seeds or nuts and serve.

Whipped Feta with Blitzed Carrots & Roast Chickpeas

I think whipping feta should go straight in at number one for the Cheese chapter of **New Kitchen Basics**. Flippant maybe, but who wouldn't want to whip their feta? This is a completely sensible way to extend the amount of one ingredient with another, less expensive one – in this case, plain yogurt. Sharp, salty feta, whipped, then tempered with the yogurt and lemon, is a terrific foil for the spiced carrots and roast chickpeas (garbanzos).

350g (12oz) carrots, peeled and cut into bite-size pieces

50ml (1¾oz) olive oil, plus extra to taste

2 cloves of garlic, peeled and crushed

1 tablespoon thyme leaves

½ teaspoon ground turmeric

1 teaspoon ground coriander

1 teaspoon ground cumin

1 x 400g (14oz) can of chickpeas (garbanzos), drained and rinsed, then patted dry

200g (7oz) feta cheese

100g (3½oz) plain yogurt

zest and juice of 1 unwaxed lemon

good pinch of chilli flakes (or more to taste)

small bunch of mint, flat-leaf parsley, or coriander (cilantro), leaves picked and roughly chopped

toasted pita or flatbreads, to serve

salt and freshly ground black pepper

Preheat the oven to 200°C/fan 180°C/400°F/Gas 6 and line a baking sheet with baking paper.

Put the carrots in a medium saucepan over a moderate to low heat, with half the olive oil, half the garlic, the thyme, the turmeric, half the other spices, a good splash of water (to stop the carrots from sticking too much) and a good pinch of salt. Cook, covered, for about 15 minutes, until the carrots are completely soft. Make sure the pan doesn't dry out, and add a splash more water, if necessary.

While the carrots are cooking, put the chickpeas (garbanzos) on the prepared baking sheet and toss with the remaining oil, a good pinch of salt and the remaining ground cumin and ground coriander. Place in the oven and roast for about 15 minutes, until beginning to colour and crisp. Remove from the oven and put to one side.

Use a blender, or large mixing bowl with a sturdy whisk, to blend the feta, yogurt and lemon zest to a creamy, whipped, dipping consistency. Leave to one side.

Put the cooked carrots, all the contents of the carrot pan, the remaining garlic and the lemon juice into a blender and blend to a coarse purée. Season with salt and pepper to taste.

Put the carrot mixture in a serving bowl and top with the whipped feta mixture and the roasted chickpeas and sprinkle over the chilli flakes. Add the chopped herbs and serve with toasted pita or flatbreads.

Leek, Artichoke & Feta Filo Pie

Pies are easy to make, and especially so when you use filo pastry. I've never really understood the scaremongering that goes on with filo pastry. Paper-thin, all these fragile sheets really need is a generous hand with the melted butter. A damp, clean dish towel draped over the sheets in waiting will help to alleviate drying out, but it's melted butter that's the real fixer. You can easily patch up any fissures that appear with another sheet and yet more butter. This pie is a knockout, with the feta baking to a gorgeous wobble along with the egg and the artichoke hearts.

150g (5½oz) unsalted butter, melted in a small frying pan and kept warm

1 x 300g (10½oz) jar of artichoke hearts in oil, drained and roughly chopped, oil reserved

1 onion, peeled and finely diced

2 big leeks, finely sliced

200g (7oz) feta cheese, crumbled

100g (3½oz) cottage cheese, ricotta, or quark

4 eggs, lightly beaten

small bunch of dill, leaves and stalks finely chopped

small bunch of flat-leaf parsley, leaves picked and finely chopped

300g (10½oz) filo sheets

salt and freshly ground black pepper

Put 1 tablespoon of the melted butter with 2 tablespoons of the artichoke oil in a pan over a moderate heat. Add the onion and the leeks and cook for about 10 minutes, until soft.

Preheat the oven to 190°C/fan 170°C/375°F/Gas 5. Line a baking sheet with baking paper and put to one side.

In a mixing bowl, combine the artichokes, the cooked onion and leek mixture, the feta, cottage cheese, beaten eggs and the herbs. Season with salt and plenty of black pepper to taste.

Lay 2 filo sheets lengthways on the prepared baking sheet. Brush each sheet with melted butter. Take 2 more filo sheets and turn them so that they are at the 11:00 and 5:00 o'clock positions, brushing each sheet you add with the melted butter. Continue to arrange filo sheets in a clockwork fashion, until you have an incrementally overlapping circle shape. Be sure to butter liberally each filo sheet as you go.

When you've used up all the sheets, place the leek and artichoke mixture in the centre and spread out, leaving a good 5cm (2in) border. Carefully fold the filo sheets over the edge of the vegetable mixture, allowing the majority of the centre to stay visible.

With the remaining butter, generously brush all the edges of the pie, then bake for 25–30 minutes, until the edges are golden and just firm to the touch. Remove from the oven and leave to cool for 5–10 minutes before slicing and serving.

POTATOES

I wasn't originally going to include a chapter on potatoes in **New Kitchen Basics**; unthinkable, I now know. It wasn't until I consulted a good friend of mine, Roz, during the research phase that the absence of potatoes came up. 'Are you crazy? Where are the potatoes?' asked Roz. 'Oh, I think pasta and rice are the more popular bastions of day-to-day cooking,' I said, a little too flippantly. 'Not in my house they're not,' said Roz, of Irish/Hebridean descent and with four kids, to boot. And on she went, reeling off a list of her favourite family potato recipes, with the buzzwords of comfort and generosity ringing clear and persistent. With our friendship in the balance, I buckled, and this is my shot at making amends. I love potatoes, of course I do (there are not many ingredients I don't); it's just that rice and pasta tend to get more of a systematic thrashing when the clock is ticking and everyone wants feeding, right there, right then. Pasta and rice can offer a reassuringly prescriptive cooking time and it's during these more frantic, ravenous moments that I sometimes find myself overlooking potatoes.

Fortunately, potatoes don't seem to mind a bit of neglect. Preferring dark, cool and dry storage, they should last for a good few months or more. Wait long enough and potatoes will sprout horny furls, in a bid to grow up again – simply cut these off and prepare as usual. Potatoes that have also seen too much light (photosynthesis… think back to those biology classes) might go a little green under the skin, but these too are fine to eat; simply peel off the pale green layer and cook as normal. I should note here, though, that any potatoes with extensive sprouting or those that have withered or turned excessively green are best avoided – deteriorated quality means loss of nutrients, and potentially dangerous levels of toxins beneath the skin.

Potatoes fall into two distinct camps – those that are fluffy when cooked (floury) and those that are waxy when cooked. You don't have to choose which sort you prefer; each has very different applications. First, there are those big, floury, cumbersome spuds, larger than your fist, good when bound for the oven to bake or into a big pan of well-salted water to boil at pace. This sort can cook to a state of collapse and are especially thirsty for fat (cheese, butter, cream, milk or oil) with the starchy flesh, then yielding, pillowy and magnificent. Mashed and roasted, or baked in their skins, floury potatoes offer up some remarkable mealtimes; they are the potatoes you want to eat when the rain turns to sleet and the smell of bonfires permeates the dark evenings.

Smoother and generally smaller, waxy potatoes sometimes go by the catch-all name of salad potatoes. With a firmer flesh and properly dense interior, these potatoes hold their form. Skin on, skin off, left whole, diced or sliced, waxy potatoes are the more reliable kind to use when you want the cooked potato to stay in shape. There is no shape shifting to be had here. Whereas floury potatoes slump immodestly into whatever fat or liquid they meet, disintegrating first at the sides before a full and final breakdown, waxy potatoes want to suck the very life out of whatever else they meet in the pan or dish. As if to shout 'give me more, more, more!', they are hungry for flavour. Throw a sprig or two of fresh mint into the pot to boil along with some new-season potatoes; minutes later, with the potatoes now cooked, you can eat and detect a captivating shiver of mint. Potatoes in curries are also a fine example – soaking up all the juices as they go about their cooking time. Super-absorbent, the culinary equivalent of a sea sponge, waxy potatoes can withstand extended cooking times, turning glossy and resplendent in many different soups, broths and braises.

This chapter, then, is for all those who might favour the modest spud, in its natural form, over other processed, shake-it-out-of-the-packet carbohydrate options. Undoubtedly, mashed potatoes, baked potatoes and roast potatoes – for these three seem to be most beloved – offer up as fine an ending as any for the potato. I don't imagine anyone really needs a recipe for these preparations; you all know them well enough – silky, smooth mashed potatoes (butter, butter, more butter, maybe some cream and a sausage, stuck in like a flag pole), baked potatoes with salt-blistered skins (an excuse for butter), and indescribably crunchy roast potatoes (duck fat, good fat and super-hot fat), these classic potato dishes are anything but new. Instead, my **New Kitchen Basics** for potatoes are an international bunch, and ones that I hope will spark fresh uses for the ever-thrifty tuber. Potatoes: Roz, I'm sorry I ever doubted you; I hope this does the trick.

Cajun Potatoes with Buttermilk & Sour Cream

Tartiflette Baked Potatoes

Sri Lankan Potato & Aubergine Curry

Hasselback Jansson's Temptation

Massaman Curry

Lemon Semolina Potato

Whacked & Drunken Potatoes

Patatas Bravas & Aïoli

Batata Vada Pav

Kleftiko Potatoes

Aloo Chaat Salad

Caldo Verde

Llapingachos

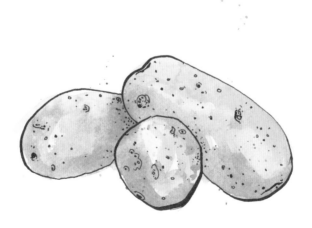

Cajun Potatoes with Buttermilk & Sour Cream

Frying the cooked potatoes in a rich assembly of butter, oil and spices ensures the potatoes suck up all the flavours from the pan. Blackening is a classic Cajun cooking method combining butter, sugar and spices, and the trio of celery, green (bell) pepper and onion is thought to be a bit of a holy trinity in Cajun cooking. I would encourage you to be bold with the chilli powder and black pepper, relying on the cool, creamy dressing to temper any fiery heat the potatoes may take on. If you can't find buttermilk, use plain yogurt thinned with a little milk to mix with the sour cream.

1.5kg (3lb 5oz) small waxy potatoes, unpeeled

150g (5½oz) sour cream

100g (3½oz) buttermilk, or yogurt thinned with a little whole milk

1 small onion, peeled and finely diced

2 celery sticks, finely diced

small bunch of flat-leaf parsley, leaves picked and finely chopped

vegetable oil

1 small green (bell) pepper, deseeded and finely diced

30g (1oz) unsalted butter

2 teaspoons smoked paprika

2 teaspoons ground cumin

½–1 teaspoon dried oregano

½–1 teaspoon chilli powder (mild or hot, as you like)

big pinch of light brown soft sugar

salt and freshly ground black pepper

Boil the potatoes in plenty of salted water for about 10 minutes, until tender. Drain and put to one side then cut into quarters.

While the potatoes are cooking, make a dressing. Blend together the sour cream and buttermilk in a bowl with half of the onion, celery and parsley, until smooth. Season well with salt and pepper to taste. Put to one side.

Put a large frying pan (or, better still, a wok) over a moderate heat. Add enough vegetable oil to coat the base, and fry the remaining onion and celery and all of the pepper for about 8–10 minutes, until soft and just beginning to colour. Add the butter, paprika, cumin, oregano and chilli, then the sugar and a big pinch of salt and pepper. Cook for 1 minute more, stirring well.

Add the drained potatoes and turn up the heat, frying the potatoes in the vegetables and spices until they too begin to take on a bit of colour. Season with salt, if necessary.

Remove from the heat, pile onto a big serving plate, add the remaining chopped parsley and most of the dressing, leaving any extra on the table for people to add more, if they like.

Tartiflette Baked Potatoes

Tartiflette is a French potato gratin dish especially popular in the mountain region of the Haute-Savoie, or basically anywhere with ski slopes. The combination of potatoes with reblochon cheese, cream, bacon or ham, onions and butter, baked and bubbling hot, is a good match for some cornichons, pokey mustard and a green salad. I've used baked potatoes here and mixed the scooped-out flesh with all the usual suspects, turning the skins into most excellent chaperones for all the cheesy weight.

4 baking potatoes

1 tablespoon olive or vegetable oil

coarse sea salt

2 tablespoons unsalted butter

2 tablespoons plain (all-purpose) flour

300ml (10½fl oz) whole milk, warmed

2 egg yolks

1 shallot or ½ small onion, peeled and very finely chopped (optional)

4 slices of smoked, cured or cooked ham, roughly chopped

200g (7oz) cheese, sliced or grated (shredded) – I like mountain melting cheese, like reblochon, raclette, Gruyère or taleggio

salt and freshly ground black pepper

Preheat the oven to 200°C/fan 180°C/400°F/Gas 6. Rub each potato in a little oil and coarse sea salt. Bake on a rack in the middle of the hot oven for about 50 minutes to 1 hour, until the flesh is cooked and the skins are crisp.

Make a white sauce. Melt the butter in a pan over a moderate heat, then add the flour. Mix well with a wooden spoon and cook for about 2 minutes, until the mixture starts to bubble, turning frothy. Whisk in the milk, bit by bit, until fully incorporated, then bring to the boil. Turn down the heat and cook for about 5 minutes, until thickened and smooth. Season with salt and pepper to taste, remove from the heat and beat in the egg yolks. Cover and put to one side.

Cut the baked potatoes in half and use a spoon to scoop out the flesh, ensuring you leave the skins unbroken. On a chopping board, roughly chop the potato and place in a mixing bowl. Add the shallot or onion, along with the ham, cheese and about three-quarters of the white sauce.

Using a spoon, carefully scoop the potato mixture back into the potato skins, heaping it in until it's all used up. Spoon the remaining sauce over the filled potato skins and place on a baking sheet.

Bake for about 10–15 minutes, until golden and beginning to bubble at the edges. Remove from the oven and serve.

Sri Lankan Potato & Aubergine Curry

In this recipe, peeled potatoes cook in the coconut milk among the aubergines (eggplants). A beautiful blend of spices brings the three ingredients together. Making the spice paste to fry along with the onion and chilli unlocks flavour like nothing else. No single ingredient should overwhelm here, with the finished curry tasting at once comforting and luxurious. Serve with rice or flatbreads to soak up the juices.

2 aubergines (eggplants), cut into bite-size pieces

½ teaspoon ground turmeric

vegetable oil

4 cloves of garlic, peeled and finely chopped

2 tablespoons finely grated (shredded) root ginger

2 tablespoons curry powder (mild or hot, as you like)

about ½–1 teaspoon chilli powder (mild or hot, as you like)

1 tablespoon white wine vinegar or cider vinegar

1 teaspoon caster (superfine) sugar

1 onion, peeled and thinly sliced

1-2 green chillies, thinly sliced (remove the seeds to reduce heat, if you like)

10 or so curry leaves (optional)

1 cinnamon stick

1 teaspoon brown mustard seeds

800g (1lb 12oz) waxy potatoes, peeled and cut into bite-size pieces

200ml (7fl oz) coconut milk

small bunch of mint, leaves picked and roughly chopped

salt and freshly ground black pepper

Rub the aubergine (eggplant) pieces with salt and the turmeric.

Pour vegetable oil into a deep-sided pan until about 3cm (1¼in) deep. Heat the oil over a moderate to high heat until the oil is hot. Add the aubergine and fry until golden brown. You may need to do this in batches. Remove the cooked aubergine with a slotted spoon and put to one side to drain in a colander or sieve (strainer) lined with kitchen paper.

Meanwhile, put the garlic and ginger in a food processor or blender with the ground spices, vinegar and sugar and blend to a rough paste. Put aside.

Place a frying pan over a moderate heat. Add enough oil to coat the base, then add the onion, green chilli and curry leaves, cinnamon stick and mustard seeds. Fry for 8–10 minutes or so, until the onion is softened but not coloured.

Add the paste to the pan and cook for 2 minutes, until it begins to stick. Add the potatoes, coconut milk and 300ml (10½fl oz) of water. Bring to the boil and taste for seasoning, adding more salt and pepper as required. Cook for 12–15 minutes, until the potatoes are tender.

Reduce the heat, add the fried aubergine and simmer for 5 minutes, until the potatoes and aubergine are both fully cooked through. Remove from the heat, remove the cinnamon stick, and scatter over the chopped mint before serving.

Hasselback Jansson's Temptation

If there is such a thing as a Jansson's Temptation pedant, then I urge them to take cover now. Erik Jansson was a Swedish religious enthusiast who travelled to Illinois in the 19th century. Eating for pleasure was a definite no-no, but this dish was Jansson's undoing. Traditional recipes instruct the cook to use sprats and very thinly sliced matchstick potatoes. However, as is the way with recipes, things changed – anchovies crept in, as did thinly sliced potatoes. One step on and here we have hasselback potatoes. You get the salty, soft-cooked potatoes plus the crunch of those spuds that have peeped just above cream level.

1.5kg (3lb 5oz) small waxy potatoes, unpeeled

30g (1oz) unsalted butter

1 large onion, peeled and finely sliced

10 anchovy fillets in oil, drained and finely chopped (or use tinned sprat or sardine fillets)

150ml (5fl oz) double (heavy) cream

200ml (7fl oz) whole milk, plus extra if needed

2 tablespoons dried breadcrumbs (optional)

salt and freshly ground black pepper

Preheat the oven to 200°C/fan 180°C/400°F/Gas 6.

Make slices in each potato about 0.5cm (¼in) apart, making sure to cut only three-quarters of the way through so the potatoes stay connected at the bottom and can fan out slightly as they cook.

Melt the butter in a pan over a moderate heat. Add the onion and cook for about 5–8 minutes, until soft and translucent. Remove from the heat.

Carefully toss the potatoes with the cooked onions and arrange the potatoes cut-side up in a large baking dish. Push the chopped anchovies into the cavities and all around the potatoes.

Mix the cream and milk together and season well with salt and pepper. Pour three-quarters of the mixture over the potatoes and sprinkle the breadcrumbs, if using, on top.

Bake the potatoes for about 25 minutes, until just tender. Add the remaining milk and cream mixture to the dish and bake for another 20 minutes, until the potatoes are fully cooked and browning at the edges (add a splash more milk to the baking dish if the potatoes begin to dry out too much). Remove from the oven and allow to rest for at least 5 minutes before serving.

Massaman Curry

This isn't a typical Thai curry preparation. The spices and flavours are more warming and heady (indicative of the migrants' Middle Eastern trade routes) than fresh and vibrant. Here, the potatoes take on the flavours of the lamb and the pungent aromas of cumin, star anise, cinnamon and coconut milk.

2 red onions, peeled, 1 roughly chopped, 1 finely sliced

4 cloves of garlic, peeled and left whole

2 teaspoons ground coriander

1 teaspoon ground cumin

1 teaspoon ground cinnamon

pinch of ground cloves (optional)

big pinch of ground cardamom (optional)

¼ nutmeg, grated

1–2 teaspoons chilli powder (mild or hot, as you like) or chilli flakes

2 tablespoons finely grated (shredded) root ginger

2 tablespoons caster (superfine) sugar

2 lemongrass stalks, roughly chopped and separated into white and green

80g (2¾oz) roasted peanuts, roughly chopped

fish sauce, to taste

vegetable oil

4 small lamb shanks or 800g (1lb 12oz) diced lamb

400ml (14fl oz) coconut milk

2 star anise

400g (14oz) small waxy potatoes, peeled and halved

juice of 1–2 limes

small bunch of coriander (cilantro), roughly chopped, to serve

salt and freshly ground black pepper

Put the roughly chopped onion and the garlic in a pan over a moderate heat and dry-fry for about 5 minutes, until softened and beginning to char a bit.

Put the charred onion and garlic with all of the ground spices, and the nutmeg, chilli powder or flakes, ginger, sugar, chopped white part of the lemongrass, 30g (1oz) of the peanuts and 2 tablespoons of fish sauce into a food processor and blend to a rough purée.

Find a pan with a lid that is a nice, snug fit for the lamb. Add enough oil to coat the base of the pan, then add the sliced onion and fry over a moderate heat for about 8–10 minutes, until soft. Add the lamb and cook for 5 minutes more, until the meat begins to colour. Add the spiced garlic and onion purée and cook for about 3–5 minutes, until it begins to stick to the pan and smell fragrant. Add the coconut milk, star anise, the rest of the lemongrass and enough water to barely submerge the lamb. Cover with a lid and cook on a low simmer for about 1 hour if you're using shanks, or 30 minutes if you're using diced lamb. (Alternatively, preheat the oven to 170°C/fan 150°C/325°F/Gas 3 and put the pan, lid on, in the oven for the equivalent amount of time.) Add the potatoes, replace the lid and return to the hob (or into the oven) for a further 40 minutes to 1 hour, until the lamb shanks are completely tender and the potatoes are cooked through.

Remove the lamb and potatoes from the pan and transfer to a warmed serving bowl. Reduce the sauce in the pan over a high heat until nicely thickened. Season with salt and pepper, then add the lime juice, and more fish sauce to taste. Remove from the heat and pour the sauce over the lamb and potatoes. Top with the remaining peanuts and the coriander (cilantro). Serve with rice.

Lemon Semolina Potato

The combination of lemon-cooked potatoes dusted with semolina (also known as 'cream of wheat') will give new definition to a tray of roast potatoes. I've sliced the potatoes here, but you could just as well cube them. You're basically after a great big plateful of rustling, lemon-scented potatoes that will suit as a side dish to pretty much anything.

800g (1lb 12oz) floury potatoes, peeled and cut into 1.5cm (⅝in) slices

zest and juice of 2 unwaxed lemons

4 cloves of garlic, peeled and finely chopped

4 tablespoons olive oil

1 heaped teaspoon dried oregano

2 tablespoons fine-grain semolina

salt and freshly ground black pepper

Put the potatoes in a pan of salted cold water. Place a lid on the pan and bring to a boil over a moderate to high heat. Simmer for about 4 minutes, until the potatoes are just tender. Carefully drain, trying not to break up the potatoes. Meanwhile preheat the oven to 200°C/ fan 180°C/400°F/Gas 6. Line a deep roasting tray with baking paper (or use a non-stick tray).

Place the potatoes in the tray and add the lemon zest and juice, garlic, a good measure of olive oil, oregano and 1 tablespoon of the semolina, along with 100ml (3½fl oz) of water. Season with salt and pepper, mixing well, and level out.

Roast the potatoes for about 30 minutes, until they begin to colour in patches with a little liquid still remaining in the roasting tray.

Turn the potatoes over and sprinkle with the remaining 1 tablespoon of semolina. Roast for another 20–30 minutes, until the potatoes are crisp and have good colour. The liquid should have all evaporated by now. If not, continue cooking until it does.

Remove from the oven and transfer to a large serving plate, scraping any crunchy bits. Check the seasoning and serve immediately.

Whacked & Drunken Potatoes

The best of cooking! Whack the potatoes until they split a bit, then drown them in a glass of wine and nearly as much olive oil to penetrate as they cook – as kitchen preparations go, this one is pretty stress-busting. Easy to assemble, it is best served warm, never piping hot, so that the flavours really sing. Use a mallet, rolling pin or the bottom of a heavy pan to split the potatoes, not in two, but near enough. Good wine – wine that you'd at least want to drink a glass of – is essential here, which is just as well because you'll be left with the rest of the bottle to drink with the drunk potatoes.

900g (2lb) small waxy potatoes, unpeeled

6 cloves of garlic, skin on

100ml (3½fl oz) olive oil

120ml (4fl oz) red wine

2 teaspoons cracked coriander seeds

2 bay leaves

100ml (3½fl oz) boiling water

small bunch of flat-leaf parsley, leaves picked and roughly chopped

salt and freshly ground black pepper

Preheat the oven to 190°C/fan 170°C/375°F/Gas 5.

Using the bottom of a heavy pan (or a kitchen mallet or rolling pin), whack the potatoes until each has split or cracked a little. Whack the cloves of garlic, too, keeping the skins on.

Put the potatoes and garlic in a large roasting tray or oven dish and add the olive oil and red wine, season generously with salt and pepper and add the coriander seeds and bay leaves. Give the pan a good mix and finally add the boiling water.

Roast, uncovered, for about 45 minutes, until the potatoes are cooked through and some have a good colour. Shake the pan a few times during cooking.

Remove the potatoes from the oven, add the chopped parsley and serve. The roasted cloves of garlic are also good to eat.

Patatas Bravas & Aïoli

In my very first job as a chef, I was the person responsible for ensuring there was enough of both the patatas and the bravas sauce to cope with demand when service started. My mise en place involved tumbling huge potatoes from a bin into an even bigger pot, then lugging it onto the stove. We made the bravas sauce in similar quantities. It was known to all of us chefs that we must never ever run out of patatas bravas – and we never did. Although we used to deep-fry the potatoes, in a domestic kitchen plenty of oil and a fierce oven will do the trick.

800g (1lb 12oz) large floury potatoes, skin on

olive oil

1 onion, peeled and finely diced

3 cloves of garlic, peeled and finely chopped

2 tablespoons sherry vinegar

1 x 400g (14oz) can of chopped tomatoes

big pinch of sugar

1 teaspoon smoked, hot or sweet paprika, plus extra to sprinkle

small bunch of flat-leaf parsley, finely chopped (optional)

salt and freshly ground black pepper

FOR THE AÏOLI
1 egg yolk

1 clove of garlic, crushed

1 tablespoon sherry vinegar

about 225ml (7¾fl oz) olive oil (use 50:50 olive oil and vegetable oil for a less intense flavour)

salt and freshly ground black pepper

Put the whole potatoes into a large pan of salted cold water, bring to a boil and cook until tender, about 20–30 minutes or so, depending on size. Drain well and leave to cool.

Cut the cooked potatoes into approximately 2cm (¾in) dice, leaving any of the skin on.

Preheat the oven to 200°C/fan 180°C/400°F/Gas 6. Line a baking sheet with baking paper.

Spread out the potatoes on the baking sheet. Drizzle over enough olive oil to lightly coat the potatoes, season with plenty of salt and pepper and bake for about 30–40 minutes, until crisp in parts and with plenty of colour.

Put enough oil in a pan to coat the base, and place over a moderate heat. Add the onion and fry for about 8–10 minutes, until softened but not coloured.

Add the chopped garlic and cook for 1 minute more, then add the vinegar and cook until the liquid evaporates.

Add the tomatoes, sugar, paprika and a big pinch each of salt and pepper and simmer for about 15 minutes, until thick and rich. Check the seasoning, adding more salt or pepper if necessary. Remove the pan from the heat and keep warm with a lid on.

Make an aïoli. Put the egg yolk, the crushed garlic, vinegar, a pinch of salt and a good dusting of black pepper in a food processor and blitz for 20 seconds. Add the olive oil (or oil mixture) in a thin drizzle, mixing all the time, until you have used up all the oil and have a nice, thick mayonnaise. If the mayonnaise gets too thick, add a splash of cold water to thin. Season with salt and pepper, then put in a small serving bowl. (You can make this by hand using a whisk and bowl if you prefer.)

Put the warm bravas sauce onto a large serving plate, pile on the hot potatoes and sprinkle over the chopped parsley. Serve with the aïoli at the table.

Batata Vada Pav

Potato mashed and spiced, then battered in gram flour and stuffed in a bun – this is a Mumbai street-food classic and one of my favourite recipes in the book. The soft white bun is entirely authentic and the object here should be how much flavour and how many toppings you can stuff in the vada before you then eat it. Pile on finely sliced red onion, pickled whole green chilli, and even Bombay mix and tomato ketchup.

400g (14oz) floury potatoes, peeled and cut into large bite-size pieces

2–4 green chillies, finely chopped (remove the seeds to reduce heat, if you like)

4 cloves of garlic, peeled and finely chopped

small bunch of coriander (cilantro), leaves and stalks roughly chopped

150g (5½oz) gram flour, or use plain (all-purpose) flour, plus extra for dusting

1 heaped teaspoon ground turmeric

2 teaspoons curry powder (mild or hot, as you like)

½ teaspoon baking powder

vegetable oil

1 teaspoon brown mustard seeds

1 tablespoon finely grated (shredded) root ginger

juice of ½ lemon

4 soft white buns or burger buns, split in two, toasted and buttered

a mixture of finely sliced red onion, pickled chillies, Bombay mix and tomato ketchup, to serve

salt and freshly ground black pepper

Cook the potatoes in salted boiling water for 15–20 minutes, until tender. Drain well and mash, adding salt and pepper to taste.

While the potatoes are cooking, blend the chillies with the garlic, coriander (cilantro) leaves and stalks, and a splash of water, to form a coarse paste. Put to one side.

Mix the gram flour with the turmeric, 1 teaspoon of the curry powder, the baking powder, a big pinch of salt and 180ml (6fl oz) of water to make a thick batter.

Put enough oil in a large frying pan to coat the base, and place over a moderate to high heat. Add the mustard seeds and fry for 30 seconds, until they begin to sizzle and pop, then add the ginger and half the prepared green chilli paste and cook for 30 seconds, until fragrant. Add the remaining curry powder and all of the mashed potatoes, season with salt, and mix well to combine. Put to one side until cool enough to handle.

For the green chutney, add the lemon juice to the remaining chilli paste and season with salt to taste. Put in a small serving bowl and keep to one side.

Divide the cooled potato mixture into 4 equal balls and pat each ball into a flat burger-shaped patty about 3cm (1¼in) thick, and lightly dust in flour.

Heat oil to a depth of 4cm (1½in) in a large non-stick frying pan over a moderate heat, until very hot. Work quickly to coat each of the patties in the batter and fry in the hot oil for about 2 minutes on each side, until golden brown all over. Remove from the heat and put aside to drain on a plate lined with kitchen paper.

Place a fried potato vada inside each buttered roll, top with green chutney – and more.

Kleftiko Potatoes

In restaurants, potatoes cooked this way are sometimes known as fondant potatoes. The potatoes cook in the liquid, soaking up the juices and turning wonderfully soft, fudgy and flavoursome. You want the finished dish to have a good few tablespoons left of the concentrated cooking juices to spoon over the potatoes, which themselves are unable to take on any more liquid. It's the sort of slow, indulgent cooking that sits well on the Sunday lunch table – with a leg of lamb or a roast chicken it would be spectacular.

about 1kg (2lb 4oz) medium-large waxy potatoes, peeled and halved

150ml (5fl oz) chicken stock or white wine

50ml (1¾fl oz) olive oil

4 cloves of garlic, peeled and left whole

1 teaspoon salt

1 teaspoon dried oregano

2 bay leaves

½ teaspoon ground cumin

pinch of chilli flakes

1 cinnamon stick

½ lemon, halved again

2 ripe tomatoes, halved

freshly ground black pepper

Preheat the oven to 220°C/fan 200°C/425°F/Gas 7.

Place the potatoes, stock or wine, olive oil and garlic in a large ovenproof dish. Sprinkle over the salt, along with a generous grind of black pepper.

Add the oregano, bay and spices to the potatoes. Squeeze over the juice from the lemon quarters, then add the quarters themselves to the dish. Add the tomatoes, and cover tightly with a lid or foil.

Bake the potatoes in the hot oven for 20 minutes, then reduce the heat to 180°C/fan 160°C/350°F/Gas 4. Uncover the dish and to continue to bake the potatoes for a further 1 hour, until they are good and soft and have caramelized in places, but are still sitting in a bit of cooking juice.

Aloo Chaat Salad

Try to get hold of chaat masala spice blend (readily available in all good Indian grocery stores, and online) for this recipe, as it will make all the difference to the finished salad. Chaat is a common Indian blend of amchoor (sour mango powder), cumin, coriander, dried ginger, black pepper, asafoetida and chilli. Mixed with the cooked potatoes, lemon, tomatoes, onion and fresh coriander (cilantro), this is a sharp, punchy jumble of a salad. Adding a good handful of Bombay mix or salted peanuts offers good crunch. A slick of plain yogurt on top would be excellent, too.

400g (14oz) waxy potatoes, peeled and cut into bite-size pieces

1 x 400g (14oz) can of chickpeas (garbanzos), drained and rinsed

1 small red onion, peeled and finely diced

200g (7oz) cherry tomatoes, halved or quartered

big bunch of coriander (cilantro), roughly chopped

juice of 1 lemon

2 teaspoons chaat masala (use garam masala and extra lemon juice if you can't find chaat)

chilli flakes or 1 finely chopped red or green chilli, to taste

salt and freshly ground black pepper

TO SERVE
good handful of Bombay mix, sev or salted peanuts (optional)

50g (1¾oz) plain yogurt (optional)

Cook the potatoes in plenty of salted boiling water for about 8–12 minutes, until tender. Drain well and allow to cool.

In a bowl, mix together the cooked potatoes, chickpeas (garbanzos), onion, tomatoes and coriander (cilantro). Add the lemon juice, chaat, and chilli (dried or fresh) to taste, and then season with salt and pepper. Overall, the salad should be quite highly seasoned.

Top with the Bombay mix, sev or peanuts, if using, and finally with the yogurt.

Caldo Verde

Caldo verde is a potato and kale soup from northern Portugal. It's a hearty number, and one to make come the colder months. I've used waxy potatoes for this soup, because I like that they can hold their own as the soup cooks out, but you could just as well use a floury spud that will break down as the soup cooks, giving a creamy, cloudy finish. If you don't want to use the traditional chorizo, by all means use good, fat, garlicky sausages instead.

olive or vegetable oil

300g (10½oz) cooking chorizo, sliced into coins

1 onion, peeled and finely diced

1–2 cloves of garlic, peeled and finely chopped (you can use more to taste, if you prefer)

500g (1lb 2oz) waxy potatoes, peeled and cut into bite-size pieces

600ml (21fl oz) chicken or vegetable stock or water, plus extra if needed

2 bay leaves

250g (9oz) kale, cabbage or spring greens, stalks removed and leaves sliced into about 1.5cm (⅝in) strips

bread, to serve

salt and freshly ground black pepper

Put enough oil in a pan to lightly coat the base, and place over a moderate heat. Add the chorizo and fry for about 5 minutes, until the chorizo is beginning to crisp and has begun to release its oil. Transfer the pieces of chorizo to a plate, keeping the oil in the pan.

Fry the onion in the hot chorizo oil for about 8–10 minutes, until soft. Add the garlic and cook for 30 seconds more, then add the chorizo back to the pan, along with the potatoes. Stir well for 1 minute or so, to coat.

Add the stock and bay leaves, along with a good grind of black pepper to season, and bring up to a low boil. Check the seasoning, adding salt to taste if necessary.

Cook with a lid on for about 5 minutes before removing the lid and adding the greens. Continue cooking for about 10 minutes more, until the potatoes are completely tender. Top up with a splash more stock or water, if necessary.

Check the seasoning. Remove from the heat and serve with crusty bread to mop.

Llapingachos

From Ecuador, llapingachos are fried potato-and-cheese cakes, served with a peanut sauce, coriander (cilantro) and chopped salsa, with quick pickled red onions and extra chilli for those who want it. This is exciting, bright cooking – the kind that is very likely to form longstanding addictions. I've said it before: be bold with the chilli – the potatoes can take it. The llapingachos are very soft to move from pan to plate, so use a good-size fish slice or something similar.

1kg (2lb 4oz) floury potatoes, peeled and cut into bite-size pieces

vegetable oil

2 small red onions, peeled, 1 finely chopped, 1 thinly sliced

2 teaspoons ground paprika

100g (3½oz) Cheddar, grated (shredded)

1 tablespoon plain (all-purpose) flour, plus extra for dusting

75g (2½oz) unsweetened peanut butter

50ml (1¾fl oz) whole milk

½ teaspoon ground cumin

juice of 1 lime

2 ripe tomatoes, finely chopped

small bunch of coriander (cilantro), leaves picked and finely chopped

salt and freshly ground black pepper

TO SERVE
Quick pickled onions (see opposite)

chilli sauce, or sliced green chilli (optional)

Boil the potatoes in plenty of salted water for 15–20 minutes, until just tender, then drain well and leave to steam dry in the pan for about 5 minutes.

Put a good measure of oil in a frying pan to generously coat the base. Place over a moderate heat and add the chopped onion and the paprika and fry for about 8–10 minutes, until the onion is soft. Put to one side.

Tip the potatoes into a bowl and roughly mash. Mix in half the fried onion mixture, then the cheese and flour, and season with salt to taste. Cover and put to one side.

In a food processor, blend the peanut butter with the remaining onion mixture, the milk and the cumin to form a sauce-like consistency. Cook in a small pan over a very gentle heat for about 5 minutes to warm and thicken slightly. Remove from the heat and keep warm.

Mix the sliced onion with the lime juice and a good pinch of salt. Leave to macerate for at least 2 minutes. Mix in the tomatoes and coriander (cilantro) and season to taste with salt and pepper. Transfer to a serving bowl and put to one side.

Make small golf-ball-size balls with the potato mixture and flatten each into a patty shape.

Dust the potatoes in flour and shallow-fry in a little oil over a moderate heat for about 2 minutes on each side, until nicely browned. Be careful as you turn the patties over – they will be very delicate. Serve topped with the peanut sauce, tomato and onion salad and quick pickled onions. Add chilli sauce or sliced green chilli, if you like.

Quick pickled onions

1 red onion, peeled and very finely sliced
juice of ½ lime
salt

Place the sliced onion in a bowl and cover with boiling water. Set aside for 5 minutes, then drain.

Return the drained onion to the bowl and pour over the lime juice. Add salt to taste before serving with a variety of dishes including the Lllapingachos (opposite), Chicken Tinga Tacos (page 24), Huevos divorciados (page 80), Sweet potatoes (page 112) and Meatloaf (page 196).

MINCED OR GROUND MEAT

I know, I know, I could have chosen a more show-stopping, singular cut of meat to feature in this book. But, in all honesty, I think catch-all minced (ground) meat is the true champ for the home cook. Go to the supermarket and chances are the chilled aisle will be jam-packed with beef, lamb and pork mince and, sometimes in bigger supermarkets, turkey, even veal and venison mince, too. Butchers, of course, sell minced meat and will weigh to your exact requirement, which is always helpful when numbers swell to feed a crowd. And while there are those who eat meat regularly, myself included, and who might like to buy and cook with more expensive cuts, it's my guess – and the guess of the supermarket executives, too – that most people cooking on a sensible budget and in an achievable timeframe buy mince.

Affordable, practical and in a reliably fuss-free form, I think the prominence of mince in so many favourite family recipes would indicate this has been the unshakable status quo for some time. The stalwarts of cottage pie, shepherd's pie and Bolognese (just three here that spring to mind – there are many more) are the unfaltering backbone of many a family meal planner. Who am I to argue?

With this in mind, and perhaps breaking ranks from other more provocative culinary iconoclasts, I am happy to declare a good and proper appreciation of minced meat. Nostalgia can run deep in food and cooking and many people have strong opinions when it comes to messing with timeworn, well-loved recipes.

In particular, recipes woven with strong bonds of heritage and tradition are among some of the most closely guarded of all. Switch certain ingredients or cooking methods around in a particular dish and it can invoke rage and a fear of change, like nothing else. Here lies the danger inherent in writing a new cookbook. With **New Kitchen Basics**, I am suggesting we move forward. If we really do all collectively roll our eyes at the thought of cooking the same dishes day in, day out (and many of these would appear to feature mince), then I think there is a case for change. It doesn't mean we have to cut loose from our favourite and best recipes, it just means we can cook them a little less often than we do. Conforming just enough, and absolutely with my Bolognese-loving children in mind, I have included a recipe for lamb ragù in the book (page 194) – made just so and served with pasta, it's a mean match for the usual spag Bol.

Top-grade minced meat, bought from the butcher or the supermarket, is also a good product for the sake of carcass balance. This is important: if there is too much of a demand for prime cuts, this creates an imbalance in the distribution chain, tipping the scales and causing unnecessary waste of less popular cuts of meat. Quality mince from a reputable source is a good way for farmers and suppliers within the meat industry to ensure that this doesn't happen and that everything worthwhile gets used. Cooking and eating meat nose-to-tail fashion, extending the amount we do buy with good cookery practice, and in this case using mince with craft and ingenuity by supplementing with additional ingredients, are thoughtful consumerist habits. I don't want to preach – that's not my business here – but what I want is to encourage people to cook great food economically and with ease. I know well the perils and pitfalls of family cookery, and drumming the new into the well-worn is this book's raison d'être. In it, I want to weave a line between authenticity and innovation. I want to tinker with some recipes, making them more appropriate for the contemporary kitchen, and I want to shed light on some more international and dazzlingly good mince-based recipes from elsewhere in the world.

Mince, you beauty. A most prudent and welcome companion for many a mealtime.

Mapo Dofu

Banh Mi

Asado Beef Burger with Chimichurri
& Mozzarella

Keema Paratha

Kofte Fatteh

Stuffed Porchetta Meatballs

Lamb Ragù with Green Olives, Peas & 'Nduja

Bobotie

Black Bean Beef Meatloaf

Meatball Pho

Algerian Meatballs with Chickpeas
& Turmeric

Mince on Dripping Toast

Mapo Dofu

A famous Sichuan mince and beancurd dish, mapo dofu translates rather unkindly as 'old pock-marked woman's face'. So the story goes, Mrs Chen was the wife of Mr Chen, a reputed 19th-century chef. A superb cook, Mrs Chen would help out in the restaurant and it was her dish of beancurd, topped with fiery hot and numbing pork mince, that drew people from far and wide to taste the dish. It is my favourite recipe in this chapter, and a good example of stretching a quantity of meat to make it go further. Sichuan pepper is a fragrant, mouth-numbing spice and is non-negotiable in this recipe. Find it in Chinese grocery stores, bigger supermarkets, or online.

300g (10½oz) firm beancurd or tofu, cut into bite-size pieces

1 tablespoon sesame seeds

2–3 teaspoons chilli flakes, to taste

1 teaspoon ground Sichuan peppercorns

vegetable oil

2 tablespoons finely grated (shredded) root ginger, plus a thin strip of ginger to test the oil

1 bunch of spring onions (scallions), trimmed and finely sliced

4 cloves of garlic, peeled and finely chopped

100g (3½oz) minced (ground) pork

2 level teaspoons cornflour (cornstarch)

2 tablespoons soy sauce

1 teaspoon runny honey or caster (superfine) sugar

2 tablespoons sesame oil

plain boiled rice, to serve

salt

Plunge the tofu into a large saucepan of freshly boiled water. Leave to soak for 5 minutes before draining well.

Combine the sesame seeds with the chilli flakes and the Sichuan pepper.

Heat 60ml (2fl oz) of vegetable oil with the slice of ginger in a medium pan over a high heat until the ginger is bubbling vigorously. Remove the ginger slice, turn off the heat and carefully stir in the sesame seed mixture. Put to one side.

Put 2 tablespoons of vegetable oil in a wok or large frying pan over a moderate heat. Fry half the spring onions (scallion), the garlic and the grated (shredded) ginger together for about 1 minute, until just softened and aromatic. Turn up the heat, add the pork mince and cook for 5 minutes, until cooked and beginning caramelize.

In a small jug or bowl, mix the cornflour (cornstarch) with 150ml (5fl oz) of water, and then add this to the pan along with the soy sauce and honey (or sugar). Season with salt, then bring the pan to the boil, add the drained tofu and the remaining spring onion, turn down the heat and simmer gently for about 10 minutes to allow the flavours to meld.

Stir through the chilli, sesame seed and Sichuan pepper mixture and the sesame oil. Check the seasoning and serve immediately with rice.

Banh Mi

French bread, Vietnamese flavours. This is a classic dish, the product of two cultures fusing in food ideology amid profound cultural upheaval. Traditionally, it would be made with a rice-flour baguette, but a common French-style baguette will do just fine. Likewise, pork pâté is often added to the sandwich; I haven't included it here for the sake of simplicity. Don't be alarmed by the quantity of sugar added to the mince – it works for good reason. Vietnamese food weaves sweetness, salt, fire and freshness with wonderful aplomb. If you plan to barbecue (grill) the meat, you'll need 4 metal skewers.

600g (1lb 5oz) minced (ground) pork

50ml (1¾fl oz) fish sauce

2 tablespoons light brown sugar or runny honey, plus a pinch or drizzle

1 teaspoon coarsely ground black pepper

bunch of spring onions (scallions), trimmed and thinly sliced

2 cloves of garlic, peeled and finely chopped

1 cucumber, peeled, halved, deseeded and coarsely grated (shredded) or thinly sliced

1 large carrot, peeled and coarsely grated (shredded) or thinly sliced

small bunch of coriander (cilantro), roughly chopped

juice of 1 lime

good pinch of salt

1 large French baguette, cut into 4 and sliced in half, or use rolls

4 tablespoons hoisin sauce, or use 50:50 soy sauce and runny honey

3 tablespoons Sriracha or another hot sauce, to taste

good amount of little gem lettuce (about 2–3 leaves per roll)

vegetable oil (if frying)

Mix the pork with the fish sauce, sugar or honey, black pepper, half the spring onions (scallions) and the garlic. Form the mixture into 4 sausage shapes, each about 15cm (6in) long. If you're intending to cook on a barbecue (grill), chill the sausages to firm up before threading a skewer through each. If frying or grilling (broiling), there's no need to skewer.

Mix the cucumber, carrot and coriander (cilantro) and the remaining spring onion with the lime juice and add the good pinch of salt and a pinch of sugar or drizzle of honey, to taste.

Spread the rolls with hoisin and Sriracha and add the lettuce and other salad ingredients.

Heat the grill (broiler) or barbecue (grill) to hot, or add a spot of oil to a frying pan. Cook the sausages for about 10 minutes, about 5 minutes on each side, until cooked through. Add the cooked sausages to the buns and serve immediately.

Asado Beef Burger with Chimichurri & Mozzarella

An asado is an Argentinian barbecue (grill). Given that it is unlikely you'll find yourself cooking this recipe in Argentina beside a fierce-hot asado, frying, grilling (broiling) or, indeed, barbecuing these beef burgers will work well enough here. What will come in handy is chimichurri, a piquant herb, garlic and chilli sauce traditionally served alongside asado meats. Mozzarella might seem an unlikely cheese choice here, but Argentina has a big Italian community, and draping a good melting cheese on top of a blistering burger is ludicrously wise. Use provolone cheese if you prefer.

600g (1lb 5oz) minced (ground) beef

2 cloves of garlic, peeled and crushed

½ teaspoon salt, plus extra to season

1 shallot, peeled and finely chopped, or 2 finely chopped spring onions (scallions)

2 tablespoons red wine vinegar

4 tablespoons olive or vegetable oil

small bunch of flat-leaf parsley, leaves picked and finely chopped

½ teaspoon chilli flakes, or to taste

1 teaspoon dried oregano

freshly ground black pepper

200g (7oz) mozzarella, sliced into about 1cm (½in) slices

TO ASSEMBLE
4 brioche buns, halved

about 2 lettuce leaves per burger

3–4 ripe tomatoes, sliced

Combine the beef, half the garlic, the salt and a good grind of pepper in a large bowl and knead very well. Divide into 4 and shape into burgers about 1cm (½in) wider in diameter than the brioche buns. Put to one side.

To make the chimichurri sauce, in a food processor or blender, blend the remaining garlic with the shallot, vinegar, oil, parsley, chilli flakes and oregano to form a smooth sauce (or finely chop and mix together in a small bowl). Season to taste with salt and pepper.

Preheat the grill (broiler) or barbecue (grill) to hot.

Grill (broil) the burgers for about 3–4 minutes each side, until crisp and brown on the outside, and a little pink in the middle (or at least this is how I like mine). Top with the mozzarella and put back under the grill or on the barbecue to melt and colour the cheese a bit – about 45 seconds.

Lightly toast the buns before assembling the mozzarella-topped burgers with the lettuce, tomato and chimichurri sauce.

Keema Paratha

These are stupendous spiced-mince-stuffed flatbreads. Paratha differs from other Indian flatbreads, like naan or roti, for example, in that the dough is enriched with fat before being rolled up, coiled round and then rolled flat again. This method helps to give the dough its characteristic open texture. It isn't tricky; just be confident in the preparation. The dough is unleavened, so it will not need proving like other yeasted doughs. Serve the parathas on their own with chutneys or as part of a larger Indian meal.

400g (14oz) plain (all-purpose) flour

1 teaspoon caster (superfine) sugar

1½ teaspoons salt

60g (2oz) unsalted butter or ghee, melted, or use vegetable oil, plus extra for brushing

1 small onion, peeled and finely chopped

½ teaspoon chilli powder (mild or hot, as you like)

1 teaspoon garam masala

2 cloves of garlic, peeled and crushed

1 tablespoon finely grated (shredded) root ginger

1–2 green chillies, finely chopped (optional; remove the seeds to reduce heat, if you like)

1 tomato, finely diced

250g (9oz) minced (ground) lamb or beef

small bunch of coriander (cilantro), finely chopped

freshly ground black pepper

In a large bowl, mix the flour with the sugar, 1 teaspoon of the salt and 220ml (7½fl oz) of water to a soft dough. Cover and put to one side for 5 minutes. Then, knead for a couple of minutes until smooth. Cover well and put to one side.

Heat 1 tablespoon of the butter, ghee or oil in a medium frying pan over a moderate heat, add the onion and fry for 8–10 minutes, until soft.

Add the spices, the remaining ½ teaspoon of salt, the garlic, ginger and green chilli (if using), and cook for 30 seconds, then add the tomato and meat and cook for 10 minutes, until the meat is cooked through. Stir through the coriander (cilantro), check the seasoning and spread out on a plate to cool down a bit.

Divide the dough into 8 pieces. Roll each into a circle about 15cm (6in) in diameter on a floured surface, then brush each with a little oil or butter. Roll up each circle, with the oiled surface on the inside, to a cigar shape, then coil up into a snail. Press down with the palm of your hand and roll each circle to about 15cm (6in) diameter again.

Spread 4 of the circles with the meat mixture. Top each with another circle of dough and re-roll to about 20cm (8in) diameter, taking care not to tear the dough.

Heat a large frying pan until hot. Dry-fry each dough sandwich for a couple of minutes, until beginning to char in places. Flip the dough and cook on the other side for a few minutes more. Place on a plate covered with a clean cloth while you repeat with the rest of the dough. Give each a brush of oil or butter before serving.

PICTURED OVERLEAF

Kofte Fatteh

Kofte is the meatball and fatteh is the toasted, crushed flatbread. Take your time over building this dish – slicking each layer as you go with seasoned yogurt and great swathes of chopped herbs. You want to make this colossal, pungent salad an exuberant, bright and arresting plateful. The meatballs and toasted flatbreads are really just the beginning, with hummus, chickpeas (garbanzos), tomatoes, pomegranate seeds, pine nuts and more all vying for attention. Dig deep.

600g (1lb 5oz) minced (ground) lamb or beef

1 small onion, peeled and coarsely grated (shredded)

1 tablespoon baharat spice blend, or use 1 tablespoon of a mixture of equal parts ground cumin, cinnamon and coriander

1 teaspoon salt, plus extra to season

4 pita, cut into bite-size pieces

4 tablespoons olive oil, plus extra for frying

1 x 400g (14oz) can of chickpeas (garbanzos), drained and rinsed

4 ripe tomatoes, roughly chopped

juice of 1 lemon

seeds of 1 pomegranate

300g (10½oz) plain yogurt

200g (7oz) hummus, shop-bought (about 1 tub) or make your own

small bunch of coriander (cilantro), roughly chopped

small bunch of flat-leaf parsley, leaves picked and roughly chopped

2–3 tablespoons toasted pine nuts or flaked (sliced) almonds

freshly ground black pepper

Preheat the oven to 180°C/fan 160°C/350°F/Gas 4.

Combine the mince with the onion, baharat spice blend and salt in a bowl. Mix well, using your hands to squish and knead the ingredients together. Divide equally into 12 pieces and use wet hands to roll into uniform balls.

Put the pita on an oven tray, drizzle with 2 tablespoons of the olive oil and toast in the oven until crisp and with good colour. Set aside.

Add enough oil to coat the base of a large non-stick frying pan. Place over a moderate heat, add the meatballs and fry, turning, until cooked through, about 10 minutes.

In a bowl mix the chickpeas (garbanzos) with the tomatoes, half the lemon juice and half the pomegranate seeds. Season with salt and pepper to taste.

Mix the remaining lemon juice into the yogurt and season with salt and pepper.

On a large serving plate, spread all of the hummus and add half the toasted pita pieces. Layer up the chickpea and tomato mixture, then the meatballs and more toasted pita, topping the layers with the lemony yogurt and a good scattering of herbs. Add the remaining pomegranate seeds and the pine nuts or almonds as you go. Drizzle with the remaining olive oil and serve.

Stuffed Porchetta Meatballs

Porchetta, a common Italian preparation, describes a boneless joint of pork stuffed with fennel seeds, rosemary and garlic and then roasted. I'm combining these same flavours here with the considerably more economical pork mince. The mascarpone melts from within, basting the meat as it cooks, making for a fine and fitting send-off for the humble meatball. Make them giant, because stuffing meatballs is a task that shouldn't take up too much time in life.

600g (1lb 5oz) minced (ground) pork

3 tablespoons fresh breadcrumbs, or about 3 tablespoons plain (all-purpose) flour

1 egg, beaten

4–6 cloves of garlic, peeled and finely chopped

2 teaspoons crushed fennel seeds

2 tablespoons chopped rosemary

1 teaspoon salt, plus extra to season

60g (2¼oz) mascarpone

zest and juice of ½ lemon

olive oil

400g (14oz) tomato passata or blended canned tomato

small glass of dry white wine, about 150ml (5fl oz)

small bunch of flat-leaf parsley, leaves picked and finely chopped

pasta, or bread such as focaccia, to serve

freshly ground black pepper

Preheat the oven to 200°C/fan 180°C/400°F/Gas 6.

Put the pork, breadcrumbs or flour, egg and half the garlic, with the fennel seeds, rosemary and salt in a bowl. Season with plenty of black pepper and use your hands to work and knead the mixture for a minute or so.

In a separate bowl, mix the mascarpone with the lemon zest and plenty of black pepper.

Roll the pork mixture into 4 giant meatballs. Stick your thumb deep into each ball to make a pocket, then fill each with a spoonful of the mascarpone mixture, sealing the hole shut by reshaping the meatball to enclose.

Place the meatballs in a casserole or roasting dish and drizzle them with a good measure of olive oil. Roast in the hot oven for 20–25 minutes, until well browned, sizzling and cooked through.

Meanwhile, put enough olive oil in a pan to coat the base, and place over a moderate heat. Add the remaining garlic and fry for about 2 minutes, until soft but not coloured. Add the tomato and white wine, season with salt and pepper to taste, then cook until thick and rich-tasting, about 10 minutes.

When the meatballs are cooked, take the tray out of the oven and sprinkle over the lemon juice. Pour the tomato sauce over the meatballs and return the dish to the oven for about 5 minutes, basting the meatballs with the sauce. Remove from the oven and serve with the parsley sprinkled over, and cooked pasta or good bread.

Lamb Ragù with Green Olives, Peas & 'Nduja

Not to replace spag Bol entirely, but certainly an excellent alternative to cook and serve with a tangle of pasta. I've added peas, olives and ground fennel seeds to the mince here, heightening flavour and texture in the finished braise. 'Nduja is a spicy cured pork paste that can give a good blast of heat to so many dishes. It keeps well in the fridge once opened and is available at bigger supermarkets and Italian delis; I've listed it here as optional, but what I suppose I really mean is, do try and track some down!

olive oil

500g (1lb 2oz) minced (ground) lamb

2 celery sticks, finely diced

1 onion, peeled and finely diced

1 medium carrot, finely diced

3 cloves of garlic, peeled and finely chopped

1 teaspoon ground fennel seeds

bunch of rosemary, sage or thyme, leaves finely chopped

1 bay leaf

50ml (1¾fl oz) white wine

1 x 400g (14oz) can of plum tomatoes

chilli flakes, to taste (optional)

100g (3½oz) peas (fresh, or frozen and defrosted)

50g (1¾oz) green olives, pitted and roughly chopped

40g (1½oz) 'nduja (optional)

400g (14oz) ridged pasta or spaghetti

finely grated pecorino or Parmesan, to serve

salt and freshly ground black pepper

Put enough oil in a frying pan to coat the base, and place over a high heat. Add the mince and fry for about 5 minutes until well coloured. Remove the mince to a plate and put to one side. Wipe out the pan and return it to the heat.

Add another sloop of olive oil and add the vegetables, ground fennel, chopped herbs and bay leaf. Reduce the heat to moderate and cook for about 10 minutes, stirring often, until rich, soft and just beginning to stick to the pan.

Add the wine and tomatoes, and then return the mince to the pan. Add salt and pepper (or chilli flakes, if liked) to taste. Cover with a lid and reduce the heat to a gentle simmer for about 1 hour until the sauce is rich and thick. Check the seasoning, adding additional salt and pepper and/or chilli if necessary.

Stir the peas, olives and 'nduja, if using, into the ragù and simmer for 8 minutes more.

Meanwhile, bring a large pan of salted water to the boil. Cook the pasta according to the packet instructions, then drain well.

Mix the cooked pasta into the ragù and serve with plenty of grated cheese on top.

Bobotie

Bobotie is one of South Africa's national dishes and not dissimilar to a Greek moussaka. I lived in Zimbabwe, Botswana and Johannesburg as a young child and remember fondly my mum making this for us. As is the way, I asked my good friend Ellen to test this recipe after I had written and cooked it myself a good few times – the apples, raisins and the milk and egg (custard with mince?!) did prompt a raised eyebrow. Reporting back with a 'delicious' from Ellen and her girls sets the record straight on this recipe. It really is all that.

vegetable oil

2 onions, peeled and finely diced

50g (1¾oz) fresh breadcrumbs

350ml (12fl oz) whole milk

500g (1lb 2oz) minced (ground) lamb or beef

3 cloves of garlic, peeled and finely chopped

1 tablespoon finely grated (shredded) root ginger

2 teaspoons ground coriander

½ teaspoon ground allspice

1 teaspoon chilli flakes, or more or less to taste

1 teaspoon curry powder (mild or hot, as you like)

1 green apple, coarsely grated (shredded)

50g (1¾oz) raisins or chopped apricots, soaked in warm water for 5 minutes, then drained

1 tablespoon red wine vinegar or cider vinegar

1 teaspoon light brown soft sugar

3 eggs, beaten

4 bay leaves

salt and freshly ground black pepper

Preheat the oven to 160°C/fan 140°C/315°F/Gas 2–3.

Put enough oil in a frying pan to coat the base, and place over a moderate heat. Add the onions and fry for about 8–10 minutes, until soft.

Meanwhile, in a small bowl, soak the breadcrumbs in 50ml (1¾fl oz) of the milk, mixing well.

When the onions are ready, increase the heat to high and add the meat, cooking for about 5 minutes to brown. Add the garlic, ginger and all the spices and cook for 2 minutes more, until fragrant. Add the apple, raisins or apricots, vinegar, sugar and soaked breadcrumbs. Season with salt and pepper and spoon the mixture into a baking dish.

Whisk together the eggs and remaining milk and pour this over the meat. Place the bay leaves on top and bake for 35–40 minutes, or until some of the patches of custard have a bit of colour and are just set – it should still have a slight wobble. Some of the custard will have seeped through the mince, fear not!

Remove from the oven and rest for at least 10 minutes to allow the custard to firm up and finish setting before serving.

Black Bean Meatloaf

I've used canned black beans for this recipe, blending half with the breadcrumbs, spices, milk and egg to mix through with the beef mince, cheese and remaining beans. Serve the meatloaf with a chunky salsa of quick lime pickled red onion (see page 175), chopped tomatoes and coriander (cilantro). Sour cream and extra chilli sauce are good, too. This is fast becoming a favourite.

3 tablespoons vegetable oil

1 onion, peeled and finely diced

1 red or green (bell) pepper, deseeded and finely diced

2 bay leaves

3 cloves of garlic, peeled and finely chopped

1 x 400g (14oz) can of black or kidney beans, drained and rinsed

60ml (2fl oz) whole milk

1 teaspoon ground cumin

½–1 teaspoon chilli powder (mild or hot, as you like)

1 teaspoon sweet paprika

1 egg

40g (1½oz) breadcrumbs

500g (1lb 2oz) minced (ground) beef

½ bunch of coriander (cilantro), finely chopped

1 teaspoon salt, plus extra to season

200g (7oz) cheese, such as Cheddar or Havarti, grated (shredded)

sour cream, to serve

chilli sauce, to serve

freshly ground black pepper

FOR THE SALSA
2–3 ripe tomatoes, cut into small dice

½ bunch of coriander (cilantro), roughly chopped

Quick pickled onions (see page 175)

Heat the oven to 180°C/fan 160°C/350°F/Gas 4. Lightly grease a 900g (2lb) loaf tin and line with baking paper.

Add enough oil to a pan to coat the base, and place over a moderate heat. Add the onion, (bell) pepper and bay leaves and fry for about 8 minutes, until soft and aromatic, but not coloured. Add the garlic and cook for 2 minutes more. Remove from the heat and put to one side, removing the bay leaves from the mixture.

In a food processor, blend half the beans with the milk, spices, egg and breadcrumbs to form a smooth paste. Transfer to a bowl and combine with the mince, the remaining beans, the coriander (cilantro), 1 teaspoon salt, the cheese and the cooked onion and pepper mixture. Mix thoroughly.

Press the mixture into the prepared tin and bake for 1 hour and 15 minutes, until cooked through.

While the meatloaf is cooking, make the salsa. Combine the tomatoes, coriander and pickled onion and season with salt. Set aside until ready to serve.

Once cooked, remove the meatloaf from the oven and leave to cool for at least 5 minutes before cutting into good-sized slices and serving with the salsa, sour cream and chilli sauce at the table.

Meatball Pho

I've blended the mince here for a characteristic uniform texture. There is a specific Vietnamese word – *dai* – used to describe the consistency of these meatballs. It translates approximately as 'chewy'. Work quickly to blend the mince, as keeping the mixture cold helps with achieving the springy texture in the meatballs. I suggest you don't shape these meatballs – rather, drop spoonfuls of the mixture into the boiling broth to encourage a misshapen form, with any smaller ones then breaking up into the pho and boosting flavour and texture. Likewise, frying off a small quantity of the mince ramps up flavour in the stock. If you can't get hold of shop-bought crisp-fried onions (bigger supermarkets, and Asian and Indian stores should sell them), you can make your own. Simply thinly slice onion or shallot, toss in plain (all-purpose) flour and deep-fry until golden brown and crisp. Cool completely before storing, if you don't intend to use them immediately.

400g (14oz) minced (ground) pork or beef, placed in the freezer for 20 minutes to firm up before using

1 teaspoon finely grated (shredded) root ginger

vegetable oil

2 tablespoons iced water

1 bunch of spring onions (scallions), trimmed, thinly sliced, white and green parts separated

¼ teaspoon baking powder

6 cloves of garlic, peeled and finely chopped

4 tablespoons fish sauce

1 teaspoon caster (superfine) sugar

400g (14oz) flat rice noodles

30g (1oz) crispy fried onions, shop-bought are good, or make your own (see recipe introduction)

1 cinnamon stick

1 star anise

In a food processor combine 300g (10½oz) of the chilled meat with the ginger, 1 tablespoon of the vegetable oil, the iced water, half the spring onion (scallion) whites, the baking powder, half the garlic, half the fish sauce, half the teaspoon of sugar and plenty of black pepper. Quickly pulse to form a smooth firm paste (or, if you'd rather, knead vigorously with your hands in a bowl). Refrigerate the mixture to chill again until needed.

Cook the noodles according to the packet instructions, drain and set aside, adding a touch of vegetable oil to prevent them from sticking together.

Heat enough vegetable oil in a pan or wok to coat the base over a moderate to high heat. Fry the remaining mince, the remaining garlic and the remaining white part of the spring onions for about 5 minutes, until the pork begins to colour and caramelize. Add half the crispy fried onions, the cinnamon, star anise, stock, and remaining sugar and fish sauce (add more to taste, if you like), then bring to a boil and simmer for about 10 minutes.

1.6 litres (56fl oz) beef or chicken stock

300g (10½oz) shredded green vegetables, such as pak (bok) choi, cabbage or spring greens

150g (5oz) bean sprouts, to serve

small bunch of coriander (cilantro), roughly chopped

1–2 limes, cut into wedges, to serve

salt and freshly ground black pepper

Use 2 teaspoons to drop small amounts of the meatball mixture into the simmering stock. Cook for about 10 minutes, until the meat is cooked through, adding the green vegetables about halfway through.

Check the seasoning, if necessary adding salt or more fish sauce and plenty of black pepper to taste. Remove the cinnamon stick.

Divide the noodles between 4 bowls, together with the bean sprouts and green bits of the spring onions. Ladle boiling meatball broth into each bowl, ensuring everyone gets their share of meatballs.

Top with coriander (cilantro) and the remaining crispy fried onions, and serve with lime wedges at the table.

Algerian Meatballs with Chickpeas & Turmeric

This recipe is broadly based on the Algerian dish of _mtewem_. It is beef- or lamb-mince meatballs served in a rich tomato sauce made with lots of garlic and chickpeas (garbanzos). I've used cumin, sweet paprika, turmeric and plenty of black pepper in the sauce, as you want it to be boldly flavoured. The toasted flaked (sliced) almonds give a welcome sweetness and crunch, and a big handful of chopped parsley at the end sweeps everything together nicely. Serve with a chopped salad (cucumber, tomatoes, red onion, cabbage and parsley is a good combination) and orange wedges.

400g (14oz) minced (ground) beef or lamb

1 large egg

6 cloves of garlic, peeled and finely chopped

2 teaspoons ground cumin

½ teaspoon salt, plus extra to season

3 tablespoons olive oil

1 onion, peeled and finely diced

2 teaspoons sweet paprika

1 teaspoon ground turmeric

1 teaspoon tomato purée

1 x 400g (14oz) can of chickpeas (garbanzos), drained and rinsed

small bunch of flat-leaf parsley, leaves picked and roughly chopped

handful of flaked (sliced) almonds, lightly toasted

freshly ground black pepper

In a bowl, mix together the mince, egg, half the garlic, half the cumin, the ½ teaspoon of salt, and plenty of black pepper. Shape the mixture into approximately 20 small ping-pong-ball-size meatballs.

Heat the olive oil in a non-stick frying pan over a moderate to high heat. Add the meatballs and fry for about 5 minutes, until browned all over. It's best to do this in batches, reserving each batch on a plate as you cook the next.

Reduce the heat to moderate and cook the onion in the same pan for about 8–10 minutes, until softened.

Add the remaining garlic and cumin, along with the paprika and turmeric and cook for 1 minute more.

Add the tomato purée and chickpeas (garbanzos) and return the meatballs to the pan.

Add just enough water to barely cover the meatballs, bring to a simmer, reduce the heat and cook for about 20 minutes, until the meat is cooked through and the meatballs are tender.

If the meatballs are ready, but the sauce remains a bit too thin, remove the meatballs and set aside on a plate. Continue reducing the sauce until it has thickened and is rich-tasting. Season well, then reintroduce the meatballs to the pan. Add the parsley and the toasted almonds, and serve.

Mince on Dripping Toast

This is robustly seasoned mince served on a firm slice of toasted bread, spread with dripping or butter (I'll leave that up to you, but dripping will reward you with a good beefy flavour) alongside a pile of peppery watercress. Mustard, pale Dijon or neon English, is also good here. I've added some rolled oats, which lend a creamy stretch to a braise. Mince on toast is as old as the hills and it's here in New Kitchen Basics because I think it's high time mince came out from under a blanket of mashed potato. Make it the day before – it will only get better with time – and assemble the mince on toast for dinner in mere minutes the next day.

1 onion, peeled and finely diced

1 leek, sliced lengthways in half, then finely sliced

1 carrot, peeled and finely diced

4 cloves of garlic, peeled and finely chopped

4–6 tablespoons beef dripping or unsalted butter

500g (1lb 2oz) minced (ground) beef

200g (7oz) canned whole plum tomatoes

2 tablespoons rolled oats

1 tablespoon Worcestershire sauce

1 glass of red wine

4 slices of good-quality bread, toasted

salt and freshly ground black pepper

TO SERVE
watercress

Dijon or English mustard

In a frying pan over a moderate heat, fry the onion, leek, carrot and garlic in about 2 tablespoons of the dripping or butter for about 10 minutes, until soft but not coloured.

Turn up the heat and add the mince, breaking it up with a spoon, and cooking until lightly coloured.

Add the tomatoes and stir in the oats, Worcestershire sauce and red wine. Simmer for a good couple of minutes, seasoning with salt and pepper to taste.

Turn down the heat, put a lid on and simmer gently for about 1½ hours (add a splash of water if the pan begins to dry out). Remove the lid toward the end of the cooking time, ensuring the sauce is rich-tasting and unctuous. As the sauce reduces it may need stirring more often to stop it from sticking to the bottom of the pan.

When the mince is ready, toast the bread and spread each slice with dripping or butter, top with the mince and season generously with plenty of black pepper, and with salt, if necessary.

Serve the mince-topped toast with a good amount of watercress and some mustard on the side.

PASTA

The classification of pasta shapes runs into the thousands. An awesome and anarchic selection, the many different forms of pasta produced in Italy alone reflect a country with a titanic spirit and healthy appetite for autonomy. Of the Italians I have met, especially those whom I have had the pleasure of cooking with and eating alongside, food (and I suppose what I'm really alluding to here is pasta) is given such great reverence in day-to-day life, I am always a little embarrassed that I don't share the same verve for a single, identifiable food source. Throughout the week, I will find myself cheerfully flitting between favourite primary ingredients, using starchy food, such as rice, pasta, potatoes, also pulses, daily and differently. Mercurial in my home cooking, I am fond too of leap-frogging whole continents to cook one dish in favour of another. In Italy, so deep-rooted is an appreciation for pasta, this staple appears to be part of the framework of family life. I don't think I am romanticizing when I say this. The gusto with which Italians consume pasta is impressive. So much so, many Italians still travel home to eat lunch, with middle schools commonly breaking in the day so that children can eat at home with their family. It is a practice I applaud. And one, I imagine, that is especially worthwhile for aging members of the population, rewarded with the regular opportunity to eat and share their day with family members.

Rooted in a practical and frugal mode of cookery (so-called 'cucina povera'), dried pasta is one such category and offers Italians a comprehensive and incredibly practical mainstay come mealtimes. It is inexpensive and quick to cook. And while I am sure Italians must cook other dishes for lunch, I've a hunch that pasta with various sauces, or in soups, is commonplace.

It used to be said that Italy could be broadly split in half – north and south – with butter and olive oil as the heartbeat to each region's cooking. I don't find that this is so true any more. The industrialization of food production, wherever you live in the world, can undermine more intimate, regional cooking practices. While this might be seen as inevitable, the nuances of food from a region or country can thankfully be preserved, in part, by thoughtful and conscientious cooking habits. Italy maintains a striking sense of regional identity in many of its most recognizable dishes. So yes, circumstances have changed in Italy, with olive oil now ubiquitous in much cooking, and no longer the preserve of southern Italy. Likewise, the Italian dairy industry, conventionally associated with the mountainous and cooler north, now thrives the length and breadth of Italy. Despite this shift, inviolable rules and long-held traditions remain in place and nothing is cavalier when it comes to the cooking of pasta. It is a national pastime, a religion of sorts.

A kaleidoscope of influence, both culturally and historically, has done little to dent the heritage of Italy's most beloved and entrenched pasta dishes. Many (and there are many) pasta dishes are served just as they've always been, from generation to generation. The shape and size of the pasta will always govern what sauce it is served with. How the sauce behaves on contact with the cooked pasta is considered fundamental to the enjoyment of the dish. Some sauces cling, slipping seductively, while others will nestle steadfast. If you thought the Periodic Table took some beating to memorize, then consider the exhaustive array of pasta shapes and corresponding sauces – so very many.

For this reason and for the purposes of **New Kitchen Basics**, the recipes in this chapter, I feel, offer a reliably authentic representation of classic Italian pasta dishes (with the exception of fideua and koshari, which spill beyond Italian borders... more on this later). Pasta, perhaps more so than any other cookery, is a doctrine I am unwilling to meddle with. Time-honoured, many of these traditional dishes are, to put it simply, unbeatable. There are many excellent Italian cookery books written by Italians; also, more recently, some wonderful Italian cookbooks written by non-Italians, the best of which all offer a true and insightful viewpoint on Italian food. My recipes for pasta offer a bloodline to some of my favourite food writers – also some of the best plates of food I have ever eaten in my life. For the sake of this book, I've made all of these pasta recipes to cook in a short timeframe and there are no baked and longer-to-assemble recipes (apologies to lasagne and cannelloni). This demarcation helps to ensure these dishes are all weeknight-friendly and ever-so quick and easy to make.

A quick word before we begin

Buy bronze-die pasta. This pasta has been extruded through
a machine and has a naturally rough and porous texture. It is
superior to cook and will behave better when cooked in water
and also in contact with sauce. It is not much more expensive,
with some supermarkets now producing their own brand. If not,
look for the blue and white De Cecco pasta packets. And, very
best of all, try to find bronze-die pasta made in Italy.

Season your pasta cooking water with a good quantity of salt,
which will mean you need to use less in the accompanying
sauce. The seasoning of the finished dish will be more
integrated, less assertive.

Pasta should come with a bite: not a firm one, but a tender one.
In particular, cook pasta al dente if you then need to mix the
cooked pasta through a sauce to coat.

Pasta cooking water is often the elusive splash or steady trickle
needed to combine the pasta with the sauce harmoniously. I
almost always will hold half a cup back to add some into the pan
with the pasta and sauce when I think the pasta needs to be a
little more fluid, a little more sublime.

I've given 350g (12oz) of dried pasta as a standard portion size
to serve 4. Appetites can swell, as can the number of people
sitting at the table, so I'll leave the more exact pasta portioning
up to you.

Milanese with Sausage

Cauliflower, Pine Nuts, Parsley & Capers

Tomatoes Cooked with Butter & Onions

Artichoke & Almond

Greens, Pancetta, Garlic & Chilli

Prawn Fideua

Asparagus Carbonara

Prawn & Courgette

Pumpkin with Ricotta, Brown Butter & Sage

Roasted Carrot Kushari

Kale & Cashew Pesto

Tuna, Tomato & Aubergine Agrodolce

Milanese with Sausage

Risotto alla Milanese is a classic rice dish from Milan. It also goes by the name of risotto giallo, or 'yellow rice'. It is a spectacular, sometimes rather gaudy risotto, made with saffron and meat stock and often served with osso bucco (veal shin cut on the cross). It's a dish that shouts proudly of the best there is from Italy's Lombardy region. Gremolata is an Italian condiment or seasoning of lemon or orange zest, garlic and parsley, often served with the risotto. I've combined those Milanese flavours with spaghetti here for a pasta dish with similar sentiments, but more achievable in a shorter timeframe.

olive oil

4 cloves of garlic, peeled and finely chopped

250g (9oz) pork sausages, skin removed and roughly chopped or squeezed out

good-size pinch of saffron strands steeped in 3 tablespoons warm water

1 tablespoon orange zest

30g (1oz) unsalted butter

350g (12oz) pasta

small bunch of flat-leaf parsley, leaves picked and very finely chopped

generous handful of grated (shredded) Parmesan, to serve

salt and freshly ground black pepper

Add enough olive oil to coat the base of a pan, and place over a moderate heat. Add the garlic and fry for about 30 seconds, then add the sausage meat and a good pinch of salt and cook for 8–10 minutes, until the sausagemeat is just beginning to brown. Stir in the saffron along with its soaking liquid, and the orange zest and butter. Remove from the heat and put to one side.

Bring a large pan of salted water to the boil. Boil the pasta according to the packet instructions until firmly al dente. Drain, reserving about ½ cup of pasta cooking water.

Toss the drained pasta into the sausage mixture, seasoning with salt and pepper to taste. Use a splash or more of the reserved cooking liquid to loosen the overall dish, if you like, and cook the pasta for about 1 minute more, until it takes on some colour from the saffron as it finishes off cooking.

Stir through the parsley, then sprinkle with the Parmesan before serving.

Cauliflower, Pine Nuts, Parsley & Capers

This is a wonderful combination of ingredients. Slow-cooking the cauliflower brings out its mellow, sweet and earthy flavour. Use short and shapely pasta such as conchiglie, orecchiette, rigatoni or fusilli. This cauliflower is also pretty spectacular simply piled onto toast as a topping for bruschetta.

1 cauliflower, broken up into walnut-size florets

50ml (1¾fl oz) olive oil

3 cloves of garlic, peeled and finely sliced

pinch of chilli flakes (optional)

350g (12oz) pasta

30g (1oz) pine nuts, toasted

30g (1oz) capers, roughly chopped

small bunch of flat-leaf parsley, leaves picked and roughly chopped

juice of ½ lemon

generous handful of grated (shredded) Parmesan, to serve

salt and freshly ground black pepper

Cook the cauliflower in a large pan of boiling salted water for 5 minutes, until soft. Drain well. Return the pot to the heat and add half the olive oil along with the cauliflower.

Add the garlic and some salt. Give the contents of the pan a good stir, put the lid on and cook for 10 minutes. Then remove the lid, add a touch of chilli to taste, if you like, stir and cook for a further 15 minutes, stirring and scraping from time to time to stop it catching. Do try to keep some chunks of the smaller cauliflower pieces in the mix – a little texture is a good thing.

Bring a large pan of salted water to the boil. Boil the pasta according to packet instructions until firmly al dente. Drain and return to the pan.

Stir the pine nuts, capers and parsley through the cauliflower. Add to the cooked pasta and check the seasoning, adding salt, pepper and lemon juice to taste.

Drizzle with the remaining oil and sprinkle over the Parmesan before serving.

Tomatoes Cooked with Butter & Onions

As pasta sauces go, this one is a coup for any cook. The straightforward sauce uses just three main components: butter, onions and tomatoes. We have Marcella Hazan to thank for its genius – the butter rounds off any sharpness from the canned tomatoes and makes for a tomato sauce with an immense depth of flavour and a silky, glossy finish. I'm not convinced enough people know of its charms.

100g (3½oz) unsalted butter

1 white onion, peeled and halved

2 x 400g (14oz) cans of whole plum tomatoes

350g (12oz) long or short pasta

generous amounts of grated (shredded) Parmesan, to serve

salt and freshly ground black pepper

Melt the butter in a heavy-bottomed casserole over a moderate heat. Add the onion halves, cut-sides down, and let them sizzle for a minute or so.

Add the cans of tomatoes, breaking up the whole tomatoes with the back of a wooden spoon. Add a good pinch of salt and plenty of black pepper.

Reduce the heat and cook, uncovered, for about 35–45 minutes, until thick and rich. If the sauce reduces too quickly, add a splash of water to the pan – it will do no harm and you want the tomatoes to have sufficient time to cook out.

Towards the end of the cooking time, bring a large pan of salted water to the boil. Boil the pasta according to the packet instructions until firmly al dente. Drain, then return to the pan.

Taste the sauce, adjust the seasoning and mix through the pasta. Serve sprinkled with plenty of grated Parmesan.

Artichoke & Almond

In a sauce that provides another classic pairing, artichokes are gently fried along with garlic, chilli and lemon zest, then combined with the cooked pasta, some peppery rocket (arugula) and the sweet crunch of toasted almonds. I would recommend any short and shapely pasta here (penne, orecchiette, fusilli or rigatoni).

olive oil

4 cloves of garlic, peeled and finely chopped

300g (10½oz) artichoke hearts in oil, drained and roughly chopped

½ teaspoon chilli flakes

zest and juice of ½ unwaxed lemon

350g (12oz) pasta

good handful of rocket (arugula), roughly chopped

4 tablespoons flaked (sliced) almonds, toasted

generous handful of grated (shredded) Parmesan, to serve

salt and freshly ground black pepper

Add enough oil to coat the base of a medium pan, and place over a moderate heat. Add the garlic and fry for about 30 seconds, until fragrant. Add the artichokes and chilli and cook for 5 minutes to allow the flavours to meld. Add the lemon zest and season with salt and pepper.

Bring a large pan of salted water to the boil. Boil the pasta according to the packet instructions until firmly al dente. Drain, then return to the pan.

Stir the pasta through the artichoke mixture, add the rocket (arugula) and the lemon juice. Serve sprinkled with the almonds, a little extra olive oil, and Parmesan.

Greens, Pancetta, Garlic & Chilli

Frying the greens in the pancetta fat with garlic and chilli is standard Italian practice for cooking many dark and wintry greens. The fat rounds off any inky bitterness and the chilli and garlic give a good and satisfying thwack. This recipe would also make a great topping for bruschetta or simply served as a side of vegetables. Use short and shapely pasta, such as mafaldine, orecchiette, rigatoni, fusilli or farfalle.

olive oil

200g (7oz) pancetta or streaky bacon, diced

4 cloves of garlic, peeled and thinly sliced

1 small onion or shallot, peeled and thinly sliced

1 red chilli, finely chopped, or 1 teaspoon chilli flakes

about 250g (9oz) cabbage, spring greens or kale, stems removed and leaves finely sliced

350g (12oz) pasta

juice of ½ lemon

generous handful of grated (shredded) Parmesan, to serve

salt and freshly ground black pepper

Put enough oil in a pan to coat the base, and place over a moderate heat. Add the pancetta or bacon and fry for 3 minutes, until the fat begins to render and the meat is lightly browned. Stir in the garlic, onion or shallot and the chilli and cook for 30 seconds. Add the greens and a splash of water. Cover with a lid and cook for 5 minutes more until the greens are well wilted, but still with some form.

Bring a large pan of salted water to the boil. Boil the pasta according to the packet instructions until firmly al dente, then drain.

Stir the cooked pasta through the greens, together with the lemon juice. Season with salt and pepper, and add a splash more olive oil, if necessary.

Serve with the Parmesan.

Prawn Fideua

Fideua is a Spanish pasta dish made using the same principles as paella. Stock goes into a wide pan to cook the grain – or pasta in this case – with some, principally the middle portion, turning soft and swollen, while the underneath and outsides (more heat, less liquid) turn crisp and best of all (if you've nailed the method), crunchy. Fideua is an excellent dish to serve among friends, with everyone digging deep from their side of the pan. While Italy may have my heart when it comes to pasta, Spain and fideua can lay claim to a portion of it. Do make the aïoli (see page 164) to serve alongside, if you have time.

olive oil

1 onion, peeled and finely chopped

1 red or green (bell) pepper, deseeded and finely chopped

100g (3½oz) chorizo, thinly sliced

3 cloves of garlic, peeled and finely chopped

1 teaspoon sweet paprika

pinch of saffron strands

1 teaspoon salt, plus extra to season

200g (7oz) canned whole plum tomatoes

350g (12oz) wheat vermicelli pasta or fideos noodles

600ml (21fl oz) freshly boiled water

400g (14oz) whole shell-on prawns (shrimp), or use peeled (mussels and small squid are good too)

lemon wedges, to serve

freshly ground black pepper

Put enough oil in a paella or sauté pan to coat the base, and place over a moderate heat. Add the onion, peppers, chorizo and garlic and fry for 10 minutes, or until the onions and peppers are soft.

Add the paprika, saffron and salt and cook for 1 minute, then add the tomatoes and cook for 2 minutes to thicken.

Add the vermicelli or fideos noodles and stir to coat well, then add the boiled water and check the seasoning. Cover and cook for 5 minutes, add the seafood and cook uncovered for a further 5 minutes, or until all the water has evaporated and there's a crust beginning to form on the bottom of the pan.

Remove from the heat and allow to rest for 5 minutes before serving with lemon wedges.

Asparagus Carbonara

This is a classic Roman carbonara reworked with some green. Use thinly sliced asparagus in season, or small, firm, thinly sliced courgettes (zucchini). The all-important pasta cooking water is the bind that brings the dish together – add just enough to combine with the egg and Parmesan so that it forms a creamy, viscous sauce that clings to the pasta and asparagus, but not so much that it turns watery. The pasta needs to be hot enough to cook out the egg, but not curdle it. Cook this with a confident insouciance and all will be well. Use linguine, spaghetti, fettuccini or tagliatelle; short and shapely pasta will also work just fine.

olive oil

200g (7oz) pancetta or streaky bacon, cut into bite-size pieces

350g (12oz) pasta

2 bunches of thin asparagus, trimmed and cut into bite-size pieces

2 cloves of garlic, peeled and finely chopped

3 eggs

generous handful of grated (shredded) Parmesan, plus extra to serve

salt and freshly ground black pepper

Add enough oil to a pan to coat the base, and place over a moderate heat. Add the pancetta or bacon and fry for about 5 minutes, until the meat is beginning to crisp and has exuded its fat.

Meanwhile, bring a large pan of salted water to the boil. Boil the pasta according to the packet instructions until firmly al dente. Drain, reserving about ½ cup of pasta cooking water.

Add the asparagus and garlic to the pan with the bacon. Season with plenty of black pepper and cook for 4–5 minutes, until the asparagus is just tender (it might need a touch longer if the asparagus stems are thick).

Break the eggs in a small bowl and whisk together with a good handful of Parmesan and a splash of the pasta cooking water.

Add the cooked pasta to the asparagus pan. Remove from the heat and stir in the egg mixture, mixing deliberately and swiftly with the hot pasta to combine. Add splashes of the reserved pasta cooking water to make a sauce.

Serve immediately, sprinkled with extra Parmesan.

Prawn & Courgette

Prawn (shrimp) and courgette (zucchini) together are a great combination. Both ingredients share a similarly sweet and firm, but tender, flesh when cooked. Here they pair beautifully, especially with the cherry tomatoes and garlic, and are especially attractive when combined with the pasta. Do try to buy prawns from a sustainable source. My preference would be short and shapely pasta here (penne, orecchiette, fusilli or rigatoni) but, equally, tagliatelle would be good.

15g (½oz) unsalted butter

4 small, firm green or yellow courgettes (zucchini), cut into 1cm (½in) slices

small bunch of flat-leaf parsley, leaves finely chopped

zest and juice of ½ unwaxed lemon

350g (12oz) pasta

olive oil

3 cloves of garlic, peeled and thinly sliced

400g (14oz) peeled prawns (shrimp; use raw and fresh, or frozen and defrosted)

100g (3½oz) cherry tomatoes, roughly chopped

salt and freshly ground black pepper

Melt the butter in a pan over a moderate heat. Add the courgettes (zucchini) and fry with a generous pinch of salt for about 5 minutes, until lightly browned and soft, but still with some crunch. Add the parsley and lemon zest, season with salt and pepper to taste, remove from the pan and put to one side.

Meanwhile, bring a large pan of salted water to the boil. Boil the pasta according to the packet instructions until firmly al dente. Drain, reserving about ½ cup of pasta cooking water.

Add enough oil to the courgette pan to coat the base, and place over a moderate heat. Add the garlic and prawns (shrimp) and cook for 30 seconds. Add the tomatoes and cook for about 2 minutes, until the prawns are heated and cooked through. Take the pan off the heat and pour over the lemon juice.

Add the cooked pasta to the prawns, then add the courgettes. Mix well, using a splash or more of the pasta cooking liquid if the dish needs to loosen a little. Season to taste and serve immediately.

Pumpkin with Ricotta, Brown Butter & Sage

Make this in autumn or winter when pumpkins and squash are in curvy, weighty abundance. Ricotta works well warmed and baked briefly on top of the cooked pumpkin and garlic to then mix through with the pasta. As for the brown sage butter, this stuff is a restaurant hack that makes almost everything taste more delicious – you have been warned. Use a short, shapely tube pasta here; rigatoni or penne would be my preference.

400g (14oz) squash or pumpkin flesh, cut into 2cm (¾in) cubes

6 cloves of garlic, peeled and left whole

about 20 sage leaves

olive oil

50g (1¾oz) unsalted butter

350g (12oz) pasta

250g (9oz) ricotta

generous handful of grated (shredded) Parmesan, to serve

salt and freshly ground black pepper

Preheat the oven to 190°C/fan 170°C/375°F/Gas 5.

Place the squash or pumpkin cubes, garlic and half the sage leaves on a baking sheet. Drizzle with oil, then season with salt and black pepper. Cover with foil and roast for 15–20 minutes, until the pumpkin is tender.

While the pumpkin is cooking, put the remaining sage and the butter in a small pan over a moderate heat. Cook for about 5 minutes, until the butter begins to foam and caramelize. Light brown sediments will fall away to the bottom of the pan and the sage leaves should be crisp but not brown. Remove from the heat.

Bring a large pan of salted water to the boil. Boil the pasta according to the packet instructions until firmly al dente. Drain, reserving about ½ cup of pasta cooking water.

On the baking sheet, mash the cooked garlic and stir through the cooked pumpkin. Add the ricotta in blobs over the top and return the sheet to the oven, uncovered, for about 5–10 minutes, until the ricotta firms up and takes on a bit of colour.

Combine the pasta with the pumpkin and ricotta mixture, adding a little of the cooking liquid to moisten if necessary. Serve spooned with the sage butter and a generous helping of Parmesan.

Roasted Carrot Kushari

A dazzling Egyptian dish of rice, pasta and lentils. The three different ingredients cook together in the one pot, giving the finished dish a wonderful stippled appearance and texture. I've served mine here with cumin- and coriander-roasted carrots, parsley, and seasoned yogurt, but it would work equally well with the tomato, butter and onion sauce on page 214.

1kg (2lb 4oz) small carrots, halved lengthways

1 large onion, peeled and thinly sliced

olive oil

1 teaspoon each of cumin seeds and coriander seeds, toasted, then ground

1 teaspoon ground turmeric

30g (1oz) unsalted butter

125g (4½oz) scrunched-up wheat vermicelli or spaghetti, or any small pasta shape

125g (4½oz) long-grain rice, rinsed in cold water and well drained

125g (4½oz) green or brown lentils, rinsed in cold water and well drained

2 cinnamon sticks

800ml (28fl oz) boiling chicken stock or water

1 teaspoon salt, plus extra to season

large bunch of flat-leaf parsley, leaves finely chopped

1 teaspoon sumac (optional)

chilli flakes (a good 1 teaspoon works for me)

freshly ground black pepper

TO SERVE
seasoned yogurt (see page 54)

2 lemon quarters

Preheat the oven to 180°C/fan 160°C/350°F/Gas 4.

Arrange the carrots and onion in a single layer in a large roasting tin. Add a good measure of olive oil and the ground spices. Season well with a big pinch of salt and some black pepper and mix well to coat the vegetables in the seasoned oil.

Cover the tin tightly with foil and roast for about 25–35 minutes, until the carrots are tender.

Meanwhile, place a heavy-bottomed casserole over a moderate heat. Add the butter, then the pasta, and fry for about 5 minutes, until lightly coloured and beginning to brown.

Add the rice, lentils and cinnamon sticks to the pasta and cook for a further 2 minutes, stirring well.

Add the boiling stock or water and the teaspoon of salt, turn down the heat and simmer, covered, for 15–20 minutes, until the grains and pasta are cooked and the liquid has evaporated. Do give the pan a gentle stir after 5 minutes of cooking to redistribute the lentils, which will have risen to the top.

Once the carrots are tender, remove the foil and increase the oven heat to 200°C/fan 180°C/400°F/Gas 6. Return to the oven and roast the vegetables for a further 15 minutes, until the carrots and onions take on some colour, turning golden in patches. Remove from the oven and put to one side.

To serve, tip the rice mixture into a wide, flat serving dish. Spoon on the roasted carrots and onions (along with all the cooking juices and all of the flavoured oil), add the parsley, sumac (if using), and a good dusting of chilli flakes. Slick with a little more olive oil. Serve with the seasoned yogurt and lemon quarters.

Kale & Cashew Pesto

Trendy vegetables don't hold much appeal for me. Has kale had its moment? I really couldn't care less. What I do know is that the greengrocers and supermarkets stock piles of this frilly winter brassica. De-stalking kale is an agreeable task – simply hold the stalk with one hand and with the other, scrunch your fingers around the leaf and rip down along the spine of the stalk, giving you the leaf in two parts and leaving the stalk behind. Creamy cashews bind beautifully with the kale here. Keep any unused pesto in a jar sealed under more olive oil in the fridge for up to a week. Use short and shapely or long pasta, as you like.

about 60g (2¼oz) kale leaves

60g (2¼oz) cashews

1 clove of garlic, peeled and finely chopped

½ teaspoon salt, plus extra to season

2 tablespoons grated (shredded) Parmesan, plus extra to serve

50ml (1¾fl oz) olive oil, plus extra to serve

350g (12oz) pasta

juice of ½ lemon

freshly ground black pepper

Put the kale, cashews, garlic, salt and Parmesan in the bowl of a blender or food processor with a good grinding of black pepper, and blitz to a coarse paste. Add the olive oil and blend to a smooth sauce.

Bring a large pan of salted water to the boil. Boil the pasta according to the packet instructions until firmly al dente. Drain, reserving about ½ cup of pasta cooking water.

Stir the kale pesto sauce through the cooked pasta, adding a splash of the cooking water to correct the texture, and the lemon juice. Check the seasoning, adjusting with more salt and pepper to taste, if needed.

Serve immediately, sprinkled with a little extra Parmesan and a good splosh of olive oil.

Tuna, Tomato & Aubergine Agrodolce

Agrodolce is an Italian sweet-and-sour sauce. Here, the vinegar and capers bring the sour, while the tomatoes and a good pinch of sugar bring sweetness. The aubergine (eggplant) lends a creaminess to the finished sauce, and boiling it rather than frying it helps with this. As for the tuna? If you thought canned tuna with pasta was a bit mass-catering pasta bake, think again. Buy the best-quality tuna your budget affords and from a sustainable source. I have been known to use either canned mackerel or canned sardines in lieu of tuna.

olive oil

1 onion, peeled and finely diced

2 cloves of garlic, peeled and finely chopped

2 aubergines (eggplants), peeled and finely diced

good pinch of chilli flakes, plus extra (optional) to serve

1 x 400g (14oz) can of whole plum tomatoes, or use the same weight of halved cherry tomatoes

2 tablespoons red wine vinegar

good pinch of sugar

25g (1oz) capers, drained, or pitted green olives

35g (1¼oz) toasted pine nuts or chopped almonds

2 x 200g (7oz) cans of tuna in olive oil, drained

small bunch of flat-leaf parsley, leaves finely chopped

350g (12oz) pasta

salt and freshly ground black pepper, to taste

Put enough oil in a large frying pan to coat the base, and place over a moderate heat. Add the onion and fry for 8–10 minutes, until softened. Add the garlic and cook for 1 minute more.

Add the aubergine (eggplant), chilli, tomatoes, vinegar, sugar, capers and 200ml (7fl oz) of water to the pan and bring to a simmer. Reduce the heat, cover and cook for about 30 minutes, until the sauce is thick and rich-tasting.

Bring a large pan of water to a boil for the pasta. Add salt.

Stir the pine nuts, tuna and parsley through the aubergine and tomato sauce and season with salt and pepper. Remove from the heat.

Boil the pasta until al dente. Drain, reserving ½ a cup of cooking water, then return the pasta to the pan.

Add the sauce to the drained pasta, adding a splash of the pasta cooking water to loosen, if necessary. Mix well and check the seasoning. Add a little more olive oil, if necessary.

Serve sprinkled with chilli flakes to taste, if you like.

LEMON

I am the woman on the aeroplane whose hand luggage is not a sleek black cabin bag, but rather a shopping bag spilling out and over; a gallimaufry of produce bought from the market that morning. I seem unable to walk past a perky, piled-high, lemon stall and not buy big. Some people buy handbags or fridge magnets or knock-down duty-free to take home, as a badge of having been on holiday. I buy lemons. At the entrance to the aircraft the cabin crew greet me – gleaming teeth – and ask for my boarding pass. They clock the well-used tote bag full of groceries; I am clutching it to my chest (like a small child, tight with reassurance). Cue bemused look to one and other, then a knowing shrug (she must be eccentric, or a chef), and on I go making my way up the aisle to find my seat. There, it gets more complicated. I don't want my bag to go in the overhead lockers, squashed and out of sight. In the bag are a couple of tremendous, triffid-like heads of puntarelle (frilly Italian chicory), a wedge of best Parmesan, a wedge of even better pecorino, a flimsy box containing some pungent salted anchovies, lardo wrapped lovingly in waxed paper, and there are lemons – lots of lemons, eight in total.

We had been in Rome for a few days, having left the children with my mum. We saw snow falling through the roof of the Pantheon, stayed up too late eating cheese and drinking wine and walked for hours each morning, bewitched by the icicles on the Trevi Fountain, stopping often for espresso.

Back to the bag, the bag is heavy. It is also a tricky, bulging shape and will not stand upright when I put it down on the floor by my feet. Soon enough, with the plane in slow motion and heading for the runway, the cabin crew come down the aisle snapping locker doors shut and squeezing bags in overhead. I look panicked and they know it: 'It will have to go in overhead,' they say. 'It can't, there's no room, some of this has to stay upright,' and, more desperately, 'My anchovies will get squashed, they will smell.' My neighbour shuffles in his seat uneasily, pre-emptively sniffing the air. I know what he's thinking (the usual – 'eccentric, or a chef').

My husband, Matt, is to my other side. We've been here before, another airport, another time, always with the same last-minute, lemon-buying frenzy from me. Hat at a jaunty tilt, neat little waistcoat, the flight attendant is still standing there. In a flash, I grab two of the lemons and shovel them in the pockets of my dress, two more I place in the net compartment on the back of the seat, two more I give to Matt with my best don't-you-dare-say-it eyes, leaving me with the last two, which I hold in my hands, like giant squeezable stress balls. With the lemons distributed, the bag is more obediently shaped and able to sit snugly under the seat in front. Buckled up, I beam to the cabin crew and listen compliantly to the safety procedure. I am a lemon pilgrim.

Back home, the eight lemons sit like great big jewels in a bowl of their own, smack-bang centre on the kitchen table. These beauties have no place in the fruit bowl. They look like a painting. Enormous great things, my Roman lemon haul have palest yellow skin, dusty like talc. They are gnarled to touch and come complete with brittle stalks and a few dark-green leaves still attached. I rarely ever see magnificent, knotted lemons like this back home. Here, most lemons come veiled in a thin coating of wax sprayed at source by the producers to help preserve freshness and protect the skin in transit. Supermarkets no doubt push for this, too, increasing shelf life, as this process must do. They are taut and freakishly smooth-shiny, like yellow patent leather. I know which lemons I would prefer to buy, given the choice.

Unwaxed lemons are available to buy, but will often come with specialist association and an increased price tag – Cook's Ingredient – or some such moniker. Uniform in size and colour, they never look like the pastel juggernauts bought in Rome or on other travels. While the wax used on wax-coated lemons is safe for consumption, most people might like to remove it rather than ingest it in any recipes that call for whole lemons, slices or zest. To do so, simply run waxed citrus fruit under very hot water and scrub with a brush. The warm fruit should then also squeeze better, releasing more juice.

Lemons, olive oil, salt and pepper are the cornerstones to my cooking. The unity of these four ingredients affords boundless beginnings and endings to so many different dishes. For the purposes of this book, with my wanting to coach new approaches for everyday ingredients, I am going to concentrate my efforts here on sweet recipes using lemons. Lemon as a condiment or flavour in savoury cooking is often more arbitrary in application, a squish here or there to brighten a particular dish, or used to ignite any richer or fattier flavours. As for puddings and baking, this requires a more exacting use of ingredients. Squishes and sploshes, even dreaded drizzles, have their place, but for the most part what you want from a recipe with sweet application is stringent direction. These 12 recipes showcase lemons in all their sour, sweet and fragrant glory.

If life gives me lemons, I have deep pockets and I always carry a shopping bag.

A quick word before we begin

Depending on use, I like a Microplane grater with a fine tooth to zest lemons when I want the zest to almost dissolve and permeate a dish. I also own a lemon zester tool, which will pare long strips of the peel away from the lemon for when I want the lemon zest to be more identifiable in a recipe, or perhaps to remove it at the end. Also, I mostly always mean a large lemon. If your lemons are on the weedy size, use two for zest but stick to the given quantity for juice.

Lemon & Chamomile Shortbread

Lemon & Bay Posset

Lemon Amaressi

Lemon & Rose Rice Pudding

Lemon Drizzle & Poppy Seed Doughnuts

Candied Lemon & Saffron Yogurt Cake

Lemon, Brown Butter & Blueberry Clafoutis

Lemon, Pistachio & Black Pepper Cheesecake

Sicilian Starched Gelato

Lemon, Honey & Thyme Madeleines

Sweet Lemon & Brown Butter Roasted Apples

Lemon & Mint Tea Ice Granita

Lemon & Chamomile Shortbread

Lemon and chamomile pair beautifully here in this buttery shortbread recipe. The shortbread keeps brilliantly; in fact, it eats better the next day, and is quite happy stored in a tin for upwards of a week. I use blitzed, dried, whole chamomile flowers, but have had equal success with chamomile from chamomile tea bags. Choose a large lemon to get plenty of zest; use two if your lemons are on the small side. The butter needs to be very soft here – a quick blast in the microwave is good… soft, but not melted.

200g (7oz) plain (all-purpose) flour

60g (2¼oz) cornflour (cornstarch)

big pinch of salt

3 tablespoons dried chamomile flowers, blitzed, or use the contents of 2 chamomile tea bags

130g (4¼oz) caster (superfine) sugar

zest of 1 unwaxed lemon

120g (4¼oz) unsalted butter, softened (it needs to be very soft)

MAKES 12 FINGERS

Preheat the oven to 160°C/140°C/315°F/Gas 2–3. Line a baking tin with baking paper. I use a square tin measuring 23 x 23cm (9 x 9in).

Sift the 2 flours together with the salt into a large mixing bowl, and add half the chamomile.

In separate mixing bowl, mix half the sugar and the lemon zest into the very soft butter, until combined. Add in the flour mixture, then gently mix, like you would for pastry, using your fingertips to form a fine, sandy crumb.

Press the mixture firmly into the lined baking tin – it should be about 2–3cm (¾–1¼in) thick. Bake in the oven for 30 minutes, until crisp on top and very faintly browned at the edges. Remove from the oven.

Meanwhile, blitz the remaining sugar with the remaining chamomile flowers (you can simply mix them together if you're using the contents of a chamomile tea bag), then dredge the top of the cooked shortbread with the sugar and chamomile mixture. Cut the shortbread into rectangles in the tin while still warm.

Allow the shortbread to cool completely in the tin before removing. The first piece can be a bit tricky to dislodge. It will be fragile. Work carefully, and store in an airtight tin.

Lemon & Bay Posset

Possets come with a frothy, old-fashioned reputation of being served, as they were a good few centuries ago, as a warm drink with a hearty slug of alcohol. Made as pudding instead, and set cold and silky smooth in glasses, the deceptively easy posset is the perfect finish to a meal. I love bay in both sweet and savoury cooking. Here, the warming, spicy scent of bay flatters the sharp lemon and sweet cream. There are many bay trees (hedges) on the walk to and from my children's school and you will often see me snapping off a small branch as I wander back home to begin my day's cooking.

2 unwaxed lemons, peel removed in thin strips (no pith), fruit reserved

400ml (14fl oz) double (heavy) cream

2 bay leaves, scrunched a little to release flavour

120g (4½oz) caster (superfine) sugar

Juice the lemons until you have 100ml (3½fl oz) of juice. Put the cream, bay leaves, sugar and zest strips in a small pan and bring to the boil, stirring a few times until the sugar has dissolved.

Simmer for 2 minutes, then stir in the lemon juice and bring back to the boil. As soon as the liquid starts to bubble up, remove from the heat and pour through a sieve (strainer) into a jug.

Divide the sieved liquid equally between 4 glasses or ramekins. Allow to cool, then chill for a couple of hours, until set. A tiny rectangle of the chamomile shortbread on page 236 would be nice served with the posset.

Lemon Amaressi

Just four ingredients here, this couldn't be simpler to assemble. Whipping the curd with the mascarpone and letting it chill for a while works magic on both ingredients. Pale lemon and lightest of light, this lemon curd mousse is impressive(-ly easy) and will have your guests wondering quite how you made it so delectably light and whippy. Layer with the cream and scrunched-up amaretti in elegant glasses or workaday tumblers for a reworked Eton Mess.

150g (5½oz) mascarpone

150g (5½oz) lemon curd

200ml (7fl oz) double (heavy) cream

100g (3½oz) amaretti biscuits, scrunched up

Put the mascarpone and lemon curd into a large mixing bowl and beat using an electric beater until completely combined (alternatively, do this in a food processor).

Pour the mixture into a shallow dish, cover with plastic wrap and chill for about 3 hours, until set to a soft cream.

Once the mascarpone mousse is set, whip the cream to soft peaks. Layer the curd mousse, whipped cream and scrunched amaretti in glasses, finishing with a dollop of the whipped cream and a sprinkle of amaretti.

Lemon & Rose Rice Pudding

Rice puddings remind me of wintry Sunday lunches as a child – also, of school dinners, both sorts (although my mum's was the superior version) baked in a Pyrex dish with dark brown and blistered skin. I hated the skin, but loved the creamy rice, all freckled with nutmeg. This is a different sort of rice pudding, made like you would make risotto – no skin! I like to serve it cold with lemon and rose syrup poured over the cooked rice. You could just as well serve it warm. Up to you.

600ml (21fl oz) whole milk

1 cinnamon stick

large strips of zest (no pith) and juice of 1 unwaxed lemon

small pinch of salt

200g (7oz) caster (superfine) sugar

3 tablespoons rose water

150g (5½oz) risotto or short-grain rice

50g (1¾oz) unsalted butter

dried or fresh rose petals (optional)

Put the milk with 300ml (10½fl oz) of water in a medium pan over a moderate–low heat, add the cinnamon stick, lemon zest and salt and warm for 10 minutes to allow to infuse.

Meanwhile, in a small pan, gently heat half the sugar with the lemon juice, until the sugar has dissolved and turned syrupy. Remove from the heat, add the rose water and put to one side.

Put the rice in a saucepan with the butter over a moderate heat and gently heat for about 2 minutes, until coated and glistening.

Ladleful by ladleful, add the warm cinnamon milk mixture to the rice and cook, stirring continuously, until all the liquid is used up, the rice is tender and surrounded by a creamy sauce, about 15–20 minutes. Give it a rapid boil towards the end if looking too soupy, but remember it will thicken as it cools down.

Remove from the heat and stir in the remaining sugar, until dissolved. Remove the lemon zest and cinnamon stick. Leave to cool.

Pour the rice into a wide bowl. Serve cold with the syrup poured over the top and decorated with rose petals, which are also nice, if you have any.

Lemon Drizzle & Poppy Seed Doughnuts

Doughnuts are not difficult to make. The batter couldn't be easier, in fact. What does take a bit of nerve, though, is the oil temperature and getting that just right. Too high and the doughnuts will brown too quickly when cooking, but still be raw and runny within. Too low and the doughnuts will soak up the oil, turning greasy and flaccid. Use a jam or digital thermometer. These sweet little doughnuts balls, drizzled with lemon icing and stippled with poppy seeds, are a triumph.

300g (10½oz) plain (all-purpose) flour

140g (5oz) caster (superfine) sugar

3 teaspoons baking powder

pinch of salt

zest and juice of 1 unwaxed lemon

1 tablespoon poppy seeds

2 eggs

225ml (7¾fl oz) whole milk

75g (2½oz) unsalted butter, melted

vegetable oil

80g (2¾oz) icing (powdered) sugar

MAKES ABOUT 40 SMALL DOUGHNUTS

In a large mixing bowl, mix together the flour, sugar, baking powder, salt, lemon zest and half the poppy seeds. In a jug beat together the eggs, milk and melted butter. Mix the wet ingredients into the dry in the bowl to form a smooth batter, then chill the batter for 30 minutes, to rest.

Pour a depth of 4cm (½in) of oil into a large, deep pan and heat to 180°C/350°F.

Work in batches, maintaining the oil temperature of 180°C/350°F and topping up with extra oil if necessary. Carefully drop teaspoonfuls of the batter into the very hot oil and fry, flipping the balls over to cook on both sides, until golden brown and cooked throughout. Test the first cooked doughnut by cutting it in half to give you a good idea as to how long each doughnut takes to cook – it should be about 1½ minutes on each side, depending on size.

As each batch cooks, remove the doughnuts using a slotted spoon and set aside on kitchen paper to drain and cool.

In a small mixing bowl, mix the icing (powdered) sugar with the lemon juice to form a paste, loose enough to drizzle. Place the cooked doughnuts on a large serving plate, drizzle with the lemon icing and scatter with the remaining poppy seeds.

Candied Lemon & Saffron Yogurt Cake

Yogurt cakes are a doddle to make. There's no creaming of butter and baking faff, simply mix wet ingredients into dry and pour the batter into the cake tin to bake. What really makes this cake special is the candied slices of lemon. Flashed with saffron, the lemon slices are first boiled in the lemon and saffron syrup and then baked into the cake, all glossy and vivid, turning chewy when cooked. I've used olive oil here as the fat, but you could just as well use the same quantity of melted butter.

175ml (6fl oz) mild olive oil, or 50:50 olive and vegetable oil, or melted butter, plus extra for greasing

2 unwaxed lemons, 1 very thinly sliced and the zest and juice of the other

250g (9oz) caster (superfine) sugar

small pinch of saffron strands

2 eggs

175g (6oz) Greek yogurt

175g (6oz) plain (all-purpose) flour

1½ teaspoons baking powder

Preheat the oven to 180°C/fan 160°C/350°F/Gas 4. Grease a 20cm (8in) round cake tin and line with baking paper.

Put the lemon slices in a small pan and add enough cold water to just cover. Bring to the boil. Boil for 45 seconds, then remove from the heat and discard the water. Put the lemon slices on a plate.

Measure the lemon juice in a measuring jug and use water, if necessary, to make up to 75ml (2½fl oz).

Pour the lemon juice and water mixture into the small pan you used for the lemon slices, and add 75g (2½oz) of the sugar. Boil until the sugar has dissolved, then add the drained lemon slices and saffron and simmer for 5 minutes, until syrupy. Remove from the heat and leave to cool.

Meanwhile, in a bowl and using an electric whisk, or by hand, whisk together the eggs, oil, yogurt, lemon zest and remaining sugar. Add the flour and baking powder and mix briefly to combine to a smooth batter.

Pour the batter into the prepared tin. Remove the lemon slices from the syrup pan and arrange on top. Reserve the lemon syrup.

Bake the cake in the oven for 40–45 minutes, until a skewer inserted into the centre comes out clean.

Use the same skewer to push tiny holes over the surface of the cooked cake and drench with the lemon saffron syrup. Cool on a wire rack before slicing.

Lemon, Brown Butter & Blueberry Clafoutis

A good clafoutis is a thing of wonder – generously studded with fruit, dense with egg, it is a firm custard of sorts, tender like a fat pancake. The batter needs to be thick enough to cook firm, still retain a wobble in the centre and not overwhelm the fruit, which sits in the batter to bake. The lemon zest macerates here along with the blueberries, and you use the juice to make brown butter, which lends a brilliant nutty and citrus depth to the clafoutis batter. Serve warm with very cold cream or ice cream.

30g (1oz) unsalted butter, plus extra for greasing

300g (10½oz) blueberries

100g (3½oz) caster (superfine) sugar

zest and juice of 1 unwaxed lemon

3 large eggs

75g (2½oz) plain (all-purpose) flour

250ml (9fl oz) whole milk, or use 50:50 milk and double (heavy) cream

pinch of salt

2 tablespoons Demerara sugar

Preheat the oven to 180°C/fan 160°C/350°F/Gas 4. Lightly grease a medium baking dish with butter.

Mix the blueberries with half the caster (superfine) sugar and the lemon zest and leave to macerate for at least 10 minutes.

Melt the butter in a small pan over a gentle heat, allow it to foam and just begin to turn golden with sediments falling away to the bottom of the pan. Add the lemon juice (carefully, it will splutter a bit). Remove from the heat and put to one side.

Whisk together the eggs and remaining caster sugar until thick and creamy, then fold in the flour followed by the milk, salt and then the melted butter. Add the blueberries to the batter and pour into the baking dish. Sprinkle Demerara sugar over the top and bake for 30–35 minutes, until golden, or when a knife inserted into the centre comes out clean. Best served warm.

Lemon, Pistachio & Black Pepper Cheesecake

Cheesecakes are best served in slim slices, leaving room for more if they're especially delicious. I like to serve this as a cake, in the afternoon with a pot of tea. The soaring notes of lemon invigorate the dense, creamy duo of mascarpone and cream cheese. You will need to cook the cheesecake in a bain marie to help to keep the cake moist as it cooks.

75g (2½oz) shelled pistachios

130g (4¾oz) plain (all-purpose) flour

200g (9oz) caster (superfine) sugar

½ teaspoon coarsely cracked black pepper

zest and juice of 2 small unwaxed lemons

80g (2¾oz) cold, unsalted butter, very finely chopped and placed in the freezer until very hard

500g (1lb 2oz) full-fat cream cheese

150g (5½oz) sour cream

4 eggs

Preheat the oven to 180°C/fan 160°C/350°F/Gas 4. Line the bottom of a 23cm (9in) round springform cake tin with baking paper.

To make the base, use a food processor to blend the pistachios, 100g (3½oz) of the flour, 50g (1¾oz) of the sugar, the black pepper and half the lemon zest to a coarse powder (you could use a rolling pin and a bag, or a pestle and mortar, to do the same job, but a blender will be much quicker and more even).

Add the cold butter and pulse (or rub in with your fingertips) to form a sandy texture. Press the mixture firmly into the tin and bake for 15 minutes or until just turning golden. Remove and set aside. Turn the oven down to 110°C/fan 90°C/225°F/Gas ½.

Meanwhile, whisk the cream cheese, sour cream and 100g (3½oz) of the sugar in a mixing bowl until smooth. Whisk the remaining lemon zest and the lemon juice into the cream-cheese mixture, followed by the remaining 30g (1oz) of flour and fully combine.

Beat the eggs with the remaining 50g (1¾oz) of sugar until pale and thick, then fold into the cream-cheese mixture.

Place the cake tin in a roasting tray and pour in the filling. Pour enough hot water into the tray to come two-thirds up the sides of the tin. Bake for 1 hour 15 minutes, until set, but still slightly wobbly in the middle.

Turn off the oven and wedge the door so it's just open. Leave the cheesecake inside for 1 hour, then remove from the oven and chill for 2 hours, or until completely cooled. Remove from the tin and slice to serve.

Sicilian Starched Gelato

Imagine strolling through a Sicilian town after lunch, where you need something to combat the fierce afternoon heat. All you want is to trail your tongue lazily through some bitter-cold gelato. Supper (likely fish, grilled) is still some way off and, anyway, you always leave space for gelato. This recipe might help you to attain this same feeling without the flights or hotels, and at a fraction of the cost. Choose a big lemon, an Italian one, for unnerving allure.

700ml (24fl oz) whole milk

3 tablespoons cornflour (cornstarch)

150g (5½oz) caster (superfine) sugar

pinch of salt

zest and juice of 1 unwaxed lemon

Whisk together 200ml (7fl oz) of the milk with the cornflour (cornstarch), making sure that there are no remaining lumps. Put to one side.

Put the remaining milk in a pan with the sugar, salt and lemon zest. Place over a low heat and bring up to a gentle simmer, taking care not to let the mixture boil.

Whisk the cornflour mixture into the ingredients in the pan. Cook over a very gentle heat, stirring, for 5 minutes, until the mixture has begun to thicken and the raw flour taste has cooked out.

Remove from the heat, allow to cool, transfer to an airtight container and chill for a couple of hours, until completely cold. Mix in the lemon juice, then freeze according to the manufacturer's instructions on your ice-cream machine.

If you have no ice-cream machine, make sure the mixture is ice-cold, then place in the freezer in a shallow container and mix vigorously every 45 minutes, until creamy and set.

Lemon, Honey & Thyme Madeleines

My granny, a proud Francophile, used to read Proust to preserve her French, as her memories of her time in the Women's Royal Army Corps in World War II slipped further away. She was an incredibly clever woman and she tried her best to get me to savour Proust's clear and beautiful prose. At the time I was too busy reading trashy teenage magazines to take her up on the challenge. I do remember, though, her telling me of the 'madeleine moment' – when the eating of these tiny cakes turbo-charged Marcel's memory to visceral delight. I've made mine with lemon, honey and thyme. What would Proust think?

130g (4¾oz) unsalted butter, plus extra for greasing

100g (3½oz) self-raising flour, sifted, plus extra for dusting

75g (2½oz) runny honey

2 teaspoons thyme or lemon thyme leaves

zest and juice of 1 unwaxed lemon

75g (2½oz) golden caster (superfine) sugar or light brown soft sugar, plus extra for sprinkling

2 eggs

½ teaspoon bicarbonate of soda (baking soda)

MAKES ABOUT 18 MADELEINES

Preheat the oven to 160°C/fan 140°C/315°F/Gas 2–3. Grease a madeleine tin – or use small muffin tins – with butter, and then dust with a little flour.

Melt 100g (3½oz) of the butter in a small frying pan and cook for a couple of minutes over a high heat, until foaming with sediments falling away to the bottom of the pan and turning golden brown. Transfer the melted butter to a large bowl, whisk in the honey, half the thyme and all the lemon zest and juice. Put to one side.

Put 50g (1¾oz) of the sugar in a bowl with the eggs and whisk until pale and thick, then whisk in the butter mixture, followed finally by the flour and bicarbonate of soda (baking soda), until you have a smooth batter. Don't overwork it – mix just enough to combine the flour and leave no lumps.

Spoon the batter into the moulds and cook for 8–11 minutes, until golden brown, risen in the middle and cooked through.

Cook the remaining butter in a small frying pan over a high heat for 2 minutes, or until foaming and golden brown. Add the remaining thyme and sugar and spoon the warm butter over the cakes as they come out of the oven, then serve while warm.

Sweet Lemon & Brown Butter Roasted Apples

These little tarts look outrageously pretty – like a rose unfurling in the heat, with the petals splaying to the point of sweet collapse. Use red apples for best effect, although green will do. Sliced thinly and encased in filo, the apples are cooked with brown butter, all spiky with lemon juice, and given a good scattering of pistachios. Serve these just warm with vanilla ice cream, Greek yogurt or crème fraîche.

100g (3½oz) unsalted butter, melted, plus extra for greasing

80g (2¾oz) shelled pistachios, or almonds

zest and juice of 1 unwaxed lemon

50g (1¾oz) brown sugar or runny honey, plus extra for sprinkling or drizzling

2 red-skinned apples, cored and very thinly sliced

4 filo sheets

vanilla ice cream, Greek yogurt or crème fraîche, to serve

Preheat the oven to 180°C/fan 160°F/350°F/Gas 4. Grease a muffin tin.

Blend or crush the nuts and lemon zest to a coarse paste, then stir in half the sugar or honey and 25g (1oz) of the butter.

Put the apple slices in a big bowl with the remaining sugar or honey and the lemon juice and toss to combine.

Use a pastry brush to butter the filo sheets, then fold each sheet lengthways twice, brushing on more butter as you go, to make one long, thin strip.

Spread the nut mixture along the long edge of the filo strips, then overlap the apple slices over the top half with the skin edge sitting just proud of the filo edge. Fold the nut-covered filo up over the apple, then work quickly to roll the whole length up from the short end into a rose-shaped loose tart.

Place in the greased tin and drizzle with a bit of the remaining butter, then sprinkle over a little extra sugar or honey.

Bake for about 30–40 minutes, until golden brown and bubbling, and the apple and filo are cooked.

Serve warm with ice cream, yogurt or crème fraîche. These are also delicious cold as a pastry.

Lemon & Mint Tea Granita

Serve this cooling, clean-as-a-whistle, lemon and mint tea granita at the end of an especially rich meal or on a hot summer's evening. I drink mint tea like it's going out of fashion: in the daytime, when I'm bored with just water, and in the evening when the last of the wine has disappeared, but I'm not yet ready for bed. A slice of lemon in my mint tea is a must, which got me thinking about freezing the mixture and serving it as granita. My children also like it when I make this same mixture as an ice lolly, suspending slices of ripe peach in the moulds, topping up with the tea and freezing until solid.

60g (2¼oz) caster (superfine) sugar

juice of 1 lemon

3 mint tea bags, or use a big bunch of fresh mint leaves

Put the sugar in a small pan with 60ml (2fl oz) of water. Bring to a boil over a high heat and boil until the sugar has dissolved. Add the lemon juice, then remove from the heat and cool the syrup.

Boil 250ml (9½fl oz) of water in a kettle or pan. Pour the freshly boiled water into a jug and add the tea bags or mint leaves. Leave to cool, then remove the tea bags or leaves from the water and stir in the syrup. Pour the mixture into a shallow metal tray.

Place the tray in the freezer for 45–60 minutes, or until ice crystals form around the edges.

Stir the ice crystals into the centre of the tray and return the tray to the freezer. Repeat every 30 minutes, or until all the liquid is crystallized heavily into icy shards throughout, but not frozen as a solid mass. It should take about 4 hours.

To serve, scrape the granita with a fork and scoop the icy shards into well-chilled bowls or glasses. Some sliced stone fruit or berries are a good accompaniment.

CHOCOLATE

'Where do you hide your chocolate?' someone asked me a few years ago now. 'I don't hide chocolate,' I answered, a little mystified. 'Oh,' she said, 'but how do you stop yourself eating it if you know where to find it?' 'But why would I hide it? Surely I wouldn't then know where to find it?' Full circle and I still find this a curious conversation. I am not a woman who hides chocolate (although I do have three children, and come a certain time in the year…).

Chocolate, it would seem, does funny things to people. Cue indulgent groans when a chocolate cake arrives on the table at a party (5-year-olds and 65-year-olds alike; it's never quite the same with a plain old vanilla sponge), or when a broken-hearted friend says all she needs is some chocolate and a good cry (although I think I might need wine and chocolate). Food magazine sales soar when the front cover features anything chocolate. Chocolate makes people weak at the knees. It makes adults, writers even, use words like 'gooey', as if chocolate has disabled the frontal lobe, the part of the brain responsible for complex thought and reasoning. 'Gooey' is not a nice word, all thick and sticky. The language of food is rife and rich and thrillingly unfettered, so I think the word 'gooey' has to go. There is one other word, and it's the white elephant on this page (let's get this done): 'chocoholic', the chocolate addict. Embargoed from here on out.

Let's begin again, without the guilt, goo and giggles. Chocolate as an ingredient has a fascinating past reaching as far back as the first millennium BC. Classic Mayan dignitaries would be buried with bowls of chocolate so that they could carry it with them through to the afterlife. The Aztecs would anoint newborn babies with chocolate on the forehead, face, fingers and toes in a ceremony resembling baptism. Aztec warriors would also be given a fortifying hot-chocolate drink before battle (curious now, when you think of all those toddlers given their cocoa-dusted babyccino fixes). Over many years, chocolate prompted prodigious trade and warfare for South American civilizations, as documented in art and literature, both indigenous and colonial. Later on, Christopher Columbus got involved and in 1502, voyaging at the behest of King Ferdinand of Spain, he captured a Mayan trading vessel full to the brim with lucrative cocoa beans. Savvy exploration, coupled with greed, it wasn't long after this that much of Europe caught on to this most illustrious ingredient. The popularity of chocolate rocketed and the celebrity of Columbus and his seafaring soared.

Which brings me roundly, albeit swiftly given the timespan and topic, to this chapter on chocolate, the last of the **New Kitchen Basics**. The introduction of cocoa, among other plants (tomatoes, chillies, corn, potatoes and more) to Europe heralded a new modern age. Fervent was the appreciation and the landscape of world food was changed forevermore. Chocolate is an ingredient that enjoys gargantuan (hysterical?) popularity. I will begin with a square of good chocolate, high in cocoa solids, all dark and brooding. I love how chocolate melts obligingly on your tongue, seductively coating every part of your mouth. It is an intensely sensory experience and there's nothing quite like it.

As for these recipes, I've picked out ingredients and flavours that I find especially flatter chocolate in all its various forms – melted, grated, chopped – and also used as cocoa powder.

There is just the one white chocolate recipe here, and I've combined it with tahini paste to temper the sweetness (see page 266). Among my favourite flavours for dark and milk chocolate are pear, hazelnut, cardamon, malt, coconut, cherry, olive oil and salt. Many of these recipes recommend a good pinch of salt; I'd suggest these pinches are intrinsic when working with chocolate, helping to boost and spark flavour.

I hope that these 12 recipes read as a love letter to chocolate. They are also all very easy to make, because I think a good pudding or dessert, like chocolate, shouldn't induce too much heartache. Quite the opposite, in fact.

Dark Chocolate Rocky Road

Malted Chocolate Bread & Butter Pudding

Dark Chocolate, Coconut & Date
Fridge Flapjacks

White Chocolate & Tahini Blondie

Fresh Mint Chocolate Ice Cream

Espresso Chocolate Fondants

Dark Chocolate, Pistachio & Dried
Cherry Torte

Chocolate Toast with Olive Oil & Sea Salt

Chocolate, Rye & Banana Pancakes

Pear, Hazelnut & Chocolate Torte

Gilled Panettone, Dark Chocolate
& Ricotta Sandwich

Salted Peanut Chocolate Fudge

Dark Chocolate Rocky Road

Rocky road, rather like flapjack, is a popular slab of confectionery. Never all that sophisticated, the traditional rocky road combination appears here, lightened as it is with a mixture of cream and crème fraîche so you can freeze it as an altogether more elegant pudding option. Try to distribute the dark (bittersweet) chocolate, meringue and hazelnuts evenly – you'll want each slice to have a good smattering.

200ml (7fl oz) double (heavy) cream

200g (7oz) crème fraîche or sour cream

350g (12oz) dark (bittersweet) chocolate, finely chopped

2 tablespoons Amaretto, frangelico, brandy or dark rum (optional)

tiny pinch of salt

4 eggs, separated

40g (1½oz) caster (superfine) sugar

150g (5½oz) toasted skinned hazelnuts

100g (3½oz) meringue (scrunched-up if large)

SERVES 8

Line a 900g (2lb) loaf tin with cling film (plastic wrap), foil or baking paper.

Put the cream in a large mixing bowl and use a whisk to beat to form soft peaks. Then mix in the crème fraîche or sour cream. Put to one side.

Melt the chocolate in a bowl over a pan of simmering water, or use a microwave on its lowest setting. Stir in the alcohol, if using, and the tiny pinch of salt. Put 150g (5½oz) of the melted chocolate to one side and keep warm.

Beat the egg yolks with half the sugar, until thick and pale, and stir into the remaining melted chocolate. Fold in the whisked cream mixture.

In a clean bowl with a clean whisk, whisk the egg whites until they form stiff peaks. Whisk in the remaining sugar. Carefully fold the egg whites into the chocolate mixture until fully combined.

Layer the mixture (roughly ⅓ each time) in the lined tin, with the reserved melted chocolate, the nuts and the meringue scattered between each layer, making sure you have enough for a generous scattering for the top.

Place the tin in the freezer for at least 4 hours, or overnight, and remove for about 30 minutes to slightly soften, before serving.

Malted Chocolate Bread & Butter Pudding

Malt loaf is wonderful stuff. Chewy with a sweet, roasted flavour, it works beautifully with chocolate. I've made this pudding often for wintry Sunday lunches and there are never any leftovers. Use vanilla or cinnamon, as you like, for the scalded milk. Bread and butter pudding is best cooked low and slow, so the custard mixture doesn't curdle, but sets to a tender wobble. Serve with ice cream, cream or crème fraîche.

about 50g (1¾oz) unsalted butter, softened, plus extra for greasing

2 x 260g (9¼oz) loaves of malt loaf, cut into 2cm (¾in.) slices

600ml (21fl oz) whole milk

1 vanilla pod (bean), split lengthways, or cinnamon stick

2 eggs

50g (1¾oz) light brown soft or muscovado sugar, plus extra for sprinkling

50g (1¾oz) unsweetened cocoa powder

SERVES 8-10

Preheat the oven to 150°C/fan 130°C/300°F/Gas 2. Grease an ovenproof dish with a little butter, then butter the malt loaf slices.

Put the milk in a pan with the vanilla pod (bean) or cinnamon stick over a high heat and heat until just about ready to boil. Remove from the heat.

Break the eggs into a bowl, add the sugar and whisk until pale and thick, then beat in the cocoa followed by the scalded milk, whisking as you go. Remove the vanilla pod (bean) or cinnamon stick.

Arrange the malt loaf slices so that they overlap in layers in the ovenproof dish, then pour over the custard. Sprinkle with a little extra sugar and place in the oven to bake for 1 hour.

Remove from the oven and rest for 10 minutes before serving.

Dark Chocolate, Coconut & Date Fridge Flapjacks

These flapjacks are excellent for lunchboxes or straight from the fridge with a cup of coffee mid-morning, when energy levels are flagging. You can play around with the spice if you like. I've had equal success with ground cardamon, and also ginger. The dried fruit binds with the chocolate, honey, coconut and oats to make this a dense and toothsome treat.

300g (10½oz) porridge (rolled) oats

50g (1¾oz) sunflower seeds

50g (1¾oz) desiccated (shredded) coconut

200g (7oz) pitted dates, finely chopped

100g (3½oz) prunes, stoned and finely chopped

200g (7oz) runny honey

4 tablespoons coconut or vegetable oil

about 1½ pinches of salt

1 teaspoon ground cinnamon

250g (9oz) dark (bittersweet) chocolate, finely chopped, or use the same weight of dark chocolate buttons

MAKES 20 SMALL BARS

Line a 20 x 30cm (8 x 12in) shallow baking tin with baking paper.

Put the oats, sunflower seeds and coconut in a dry frying pan over a high heat and toast for 5 minutes, until just beginning to turn golden brown. Remove to a large bowl.

Put the dates, half the prunes, the honey and half the coconut or vegetable oil with 1 pinch of salt in a food processor and blitz to a thick purée.

Add the purée to the toasted oat mixture. Add the cinnamon, half the chocolate, and the remaining prunes, and use your hands to completely combine.

Tip the mixture into the prepared baking tin and press it out until it is even and level.

Melt the remaining chocolate and remaining coconut or vegetable oil in a bowl over a pan of simmering water, or use a microwave on its lowest setting. Remove from the heat, stir in a tiny pinch of salt and leave to cool slightly. Drizzle the mixture over the top of the flapjack in a lacy pattern.

Put the flapjack in the fridge for 2 hours, until set, then turn out and slice into bars.

White Chocolate & Tahini Blondie

Brownies are old hat! Blondies are the new brownies… Or something like that! White chocolate can be indescribably sweet, so I've added tahini here for its savoury, nutty charms. Cut into small squares, this white chocolate and tahini blondie is knock-out delicious. Black sesame seeds still have their hulls intact and give a pretty jet-black freckle to so many dishes. White sesame seeds are just as good – a mixture of the two is perfect. The blondie will keep for 5 days in a sealed container. I find it eats even better the day after it is made.

250g (9oz) unsalted butter

250g (9oz) white chocolate

4 eggs

150g (5½oz) light brown soft sugar

150g (5½oz) tahini paste

120g (4¼oz) spelt or plain (all-purpose) flour, sifted

½ teaspoon sea salt

2 tablespoons mixed black and white sesame seeds, plus extra for sprinkling

MAKES 16 SQUARES

Preheat the oven to 180°C/fan 160°C/350°F/Gas 4. Line a 21 x 21cm (8¼ x 8¼in) baking tin with baking paper.

Melt the butter and white chocolate in a bowl over a pan of gently simmering water, or use a microwave on its lowest setting, stirring a few times. Once melted, leave to cool for 5 minutes.

Crack the eggs into a large bowl, add the sugar and whisk together until thick and pale.

Add the tahini to the melted chocolate and give it a good stir – don't worry if it separates. Mix the chocolate mixture into the whisked eggs, until fully combined, then fold in the flour, salt and sesame seeds. Stir until no traces of flour remain.

Pour the mixture into the prepared tin, smoothing it into the corners, and sprinkle over a few extra sesame seeds. Bake for 25–30 minutes, until firm on top, but still with a slight wobble in the centre.

Cool completely in the tin – the blondies will sink in the middle as they cool – and cut into 16 squares before removing.

Fresh Mint Chocolate Ice Cream

I have a small domestic ice-cream churner that didn't cost much and makes superb ice cream in small batches. I've used the Italian stracciatella method here of pouring in (in this case) melted chocolate at the very last minute, so that the warm chocolate solidifies in strands through the cold custard mixture. The fresh mint flavour lingers long in this ice cream. Find a good and pungent mint if you can.

400ml (14fl oz) double (heavy) cream

200ml (7fl oz) whole milk

large bunch of mint, leaves picked

tiny pinch of salt

4 egg yolks

60g (2¼oz) caster (superfine) sugar

100g (3½oz) dark (bittersweet) chocolate

1 teaspoon vegetable oil

SERVES 8

Pour the cream and milk into a pan and place over a high heat. Bring up to just under a boil, then remove from the heat and stir in the mint leaves and the tiny pinch of salt. Cover and leave to infuse for 1 hour.

Whisk together the egg yolks and sugar until thick and pale.

Strain the cream mixture into a jug, pressing as much flavoured cream out of the leaves as you can. Put the egg yolk mixture into a large pan, then pour in the minty cream and stir to combine.

Place the pan over a medium to low heat, and gradually cook the custard, whisking often, until the custard has thickened enough to coat the back of a wooden spoon. If you run your finger along the coated spoon it should leave a clean line. (Alternatively, if you have a cooking thermometer, the temperature of the mixture should reach 75°C/167°F.)

Strain the custard through a sieve into a container and allow to cool a bit before placing in the fridge for a few hours until completely chilled.

Transfer the mixture into your ice-cream machine and churn according to the manufacturer's instructions.

While the ice cream churns, melt the chocolate in a bowl over a pan of simmering water, or in a microwave on its lowest setting, and stir in the oil. Allow the mixture to cool slightly.

Once the ice cream is almost churned and it looks thick, frozen and creamy, with the motor still running, drizzle in the melted chocolate. Transfer the churned ice cream to a tub and freeze for at least 2 hours before serving.

Espresso Chocolate Fondants

Freshly brewed coffee is pretty much essential here. If you don't have a coffee machine that makes espresso, by all means make strong black coffee with a cafetière or similar (I use an aeropress). This is a brooding and stylish pudding option. I serve these molten from the oven with vanilla ice cream and extra espresso to pour at the table. For a good restaurant hack, you can prepare these pots ahead of time and freeze them to bake straight from the freezer, making this a canny pudding to make with minimal effort come crunch time.

100g (3½oz) unsalted butter, plus extra, melted, for brushing

2 teaspoons unsweetened cocoa powder, for coating

120g (4½oz) dark (bittersweet) chocolate, chopped

1 tablespoon espresso or strong black coffee

pinch of salt

1 egg, plus 3 yolks

100g (3½oz) caster (superfine) sugar

100g (3½oz) plain (all-purpose) flour

vanilla ice cream, to serve

Preheat the oven to 200°C/fan 180°C/400°F/Gas 6. Brush 4 x 150ml (5½fl oz) dariole moulds with melted butter. Add ½ a teaspoon of cocoa to each basin and rotate to coat the inside.

Melt the chocolate with the butter in a bowl over a pan of simmering water, or use a microwave on its lowest setting. Remove from the heat, and stir in the espresso. Add the salt and leave to cool slightly.

Crack the egg into a bowl, add the 3 egg yolks and the sugar and whisk until pale and thick. Fold the egg mixture into the melted chocolate. Fold in the flour until fully combined and divide the mixture equally between the darioles.

Bake on a baking sheet for 10–12 minutes, until the tops have formed a crust and they are starting to come away from the sides of their moulds. Remove from the oven and tip out of the moulds to serve.

TIP: To cook from frozen, bake straight from the freezer for 18–20 minutes at 200°C/fan 180°C/400°F/Gas 6, until firm to touch but still molten within.

Dark Chocolate, Pistachio & Dried Cherry Torte

Dried cherries are one of my favourite dried fruits; sour, sweet and wilfully chewy, their inclusion here along with pistachios, cardamon and chocolate is spot on. What makes this cake especially clever is how the cake batter behaves as it bakes. On the bottom you get a good crunchy base, and the remaining half of the base is then mixed through with the sour cream and egg to bake as a soft and cake-y top, all studded with nuts, cherries and chocolate. Serve with crème fraîche or sour cream.

130g (4¾oz) light brown soft sugar, plus 2 tablespoons for sprinkling

½ teaspoon ground cinnamon

½ teaspoon ground cardamon

100g (3½oz) plain (all-purpose) flour

pinch of salt

50g (1¾oz) cold unsalted butter, diced

1 tablespoon unsweetened cocoa powder

120ml (4fl oz) sour cream, plus extra to serve

½ teaspoon baking powder

1 egg

80g (2¾oz) dark (bittersweet) chocolate, finely chopped, or use the same weight of dark chocolate buttons

40g (1½oz) shelled pistachios or chopped almonds

40g (1½oz) dried cherries

SERVES 8

Preheat the oven to 180°C/fan 160°C/350°F/Gas 4. Line a 24cm (9½in) round cake tin with baking paper.

Combine the sugar, spices and flour with the pinch of salt in a large mixing bowl. Rub in the butter using your fingertips, until you have a sandy texture. (Alternatively, you can do this bit in a food processor, pulsing until you have the right texture.) Tip half the mixture into a separate bowl and stir in the cocoa. Transfer the mixture to the prepared cake tin and press down slightly to form an even base.

In a separate bowl, whisk together the sour cream, baking powder and egg. Add this to the remaining flour mixture, then stir in the chocolate, pistachios and dried cherries, and pour the whole lot over the pressed base. Sprinkle the mixture with the 2 tablespoons of sugar.

Bake for 40 minutes, until golden on top and a skewer inserted into the centre comes out clean. Remove from the oven and allow the torte to cool in the tin for 10 minutes, then turn out and slice.

Chocolate Toast with Olive Oil & Sea Salt

Less of a pudding and more of a late-night snack to be eaten standing up in the kitchen, ready for round two, this is delicious and a complete doddle to assemble. Use good-quality, best-you-can-buy chocolate, likewise olive oil and bread. The magic here lies in so few ingredients and so little preparation. I might be inclined to serve this with a small glass of off-dry sherry; an oloroso or Pedro Ximénez would be fantastic, complementing the salt, olive oil and, of course, dark (bittersweet) chocolate.

4 thick slices of sourdough or other good, robust bread

150g (5½oz) dark (bittersweet) chocolate, grated (shredded)

3 tablespoons best-quality olive oil, plus extra to serve

good pinch of sea salt flakes (kosher salt)

SERVES 4

Toast the bread, then immediately distribute the grated (shredded) chocolate over the hot toast. Drizzle each slice with olive oil and add a good pinch of salt. Serve immediately.

Chocolate, Rye & Banana Pancakes

A weekend without pancakes is not a weekend in my children's eyes. They are the very essence of kitchen basic. This version is made with cocoa and rye flour for a change. It is a swift recipe to assemble, taking almost no time at all. Blending very ripe bananas into the mixture makes for a naturally sweet pancake batter. I serve these little pancakes with sliced bananas, some maple syrup, a handful of chopped almonds or hazelnuts, and a blob of good, thick plain yogurt. Strawberries or raspberries would be equally good, maybe with some ice cream, too.

2 bananas, peeled and chopped, plus extra to serve

3 eggs

3 tablespoons unsweetened cocoa powder

3 tablespoons light brown soft sugar

60ml (2¼fl oz) whole milk

pinch of salt

60g (2¼oz) rye or spelt flour

20g (¾oz) porridge (rolled) oats

unsalted butter, for frying

TO SERVE
maple syrup or runny honey

handful of chopped nuts

Use a food processor or blender to blend the bananas, eggs, cocoa powder, sugar, milk and salt until smooth.

Transfer the mixture to a bowl and stir in the rye flour and oats until well combined. Allow the batter to stand for 5 minutes, until thickened slightly.

Heat a nonstick frying pan over medium heat. Melt a little butter in the pan and add spoonfuls of the batter, frying in batches for about 2–3 minutes, until dark brown on both sides. Serve the pancakes with a drizzle of maple syrup or honey, more banana slices and a scattering of nuts on top.

Pear, Hazelnut & Chocolate Torte

Pear with chocolate is a classic combination and a French one at that. Poires Belle Hélène, named after the operetta Belle Hélène, was developed in 1864 by none other than the mighty Auguste Escoffier (whose name gave us 'scoffing'). The combination is reimagined here in cake form with hazelnuts. I think Escoffier would be happy with this. It is a flourless cake and has a lean cooking time, because I wanted the chocolate to slump among the pears, turning dense and delicious. The hazelnuts lend a sweet, assertive crunch. This cake keeps well for a good few days if stored in the fridge.

90g (3¼oz) skinned hazelnuts

90g (3¼oz) dark (bittersweet) chocolate, broken into pieces

90g (3¼oz) unsalted butter

pinch of salt

3 eggs, separated

90g (3¼oz) caster (superfine) sugar

2 ripe pears, peeled, cored and each cut into 6

crème fraîche, cream or vanilla ice cream, to serve

SERVES 6–8

Preheat the oven to 180°C/fan 160°C/350°F/Gas 4. Line a 25cm (10in) loose-bottomed round cake tin with baking paper.

Toast the hazelnuts in a baking dish in the oven for 10 minutes, until golden, then finely chop or pulse in a food processor to a coarse powder.

Melt the chocolate and butter in a bowl over a pan of simmering water, or use a microwave on a low setting, add the salt and put to one side to cool slightly.

Whisk the egg yolks with the sugar until pale and thick. Fold the egg mixture into the melted chocolate, followed by the hazelnuts.

In a separate bowl, with a clean whisk, beat the egg whites to form soft peaks. Stir a tablespoon of the whisked egg whites into the chocolate mixture to loosen, then gently fold in the remaining egg whites until no streaks remain. Pour the mixture into the prepared tin and level out, then arrange the pears on top.

Bake for about 20–25 minutes, until the cake is just set, with the middle looking slightly wobbly or underdone. Leave the cake to cool in the tin slightly before turning out onto a wire rack to cool completely.

Grilled Panettone, Dark Chocolate & Ricotta Sandwich

Panettone is an Italian sweet-yeasted bread studded with dried fruit. It is prolific in the shops come Christmas time. Traditionally, it is served in slices and dunked into small glasses of sweet wine. This recipe is a good way of using up any dry panettone. The chocolate and ricotta soften between the hot slices. It is a fried cheese sandwich of sweet proportion – and, in my book, a good thing to eat any time of the year. You could use fruit bread in lieu of panettone, if you like.

250g (9oz) ricotta

30g (1oz) icing (powdered) sugar, plus extra for dusting

100g (3½oz) dark (bittersweet) chocolate, coarsely grated (shredded)

50g (1¾oz) almonds, chopped

50g (1¾oz) dried cranberries or cherries, or currants

1–2 tablespoons Marsala, Amaretto, rum or brandy (optional)

8 good slices of panettone, buttered on both sides

In a bowl, mix the ricotta with the icing (powdered) sugar, chocolate, almonds, dried fruit and alcohol (if using) and set to one side.

In a dry frying pan or under a hot grill (broiler), toast the panettone slices, until crisp and golden.

Work quickly to assemble the sandwiches. Divide the ricotta and chocolate mixture between 4 slices of panettone and top with the remaining slices, sandwiching the mixture between them.

Briefly grill (broil) or fry the sandwiches for about 45 seconds on each side, flipping carefully. Serve immediately.

Salted Peanut Chocolate Fudge

Adding salt to fudge, like adding salt to caramel, should really be compulsory. Salt helps to carve an agreeable path through many different sweet recipes, often enhancing accompanying flavours. Without salt, many confections can taste overwhelmingly sweet and one-dimensional. The popularity of salted caramel confirms this. Here, with the chocolate, this salted fudge is shamefully addictive.

130g (4¾oz) unsalted butter

400g (14oz) light muscovado or dark brown soft sugar

120ml (4fl oz) whole milk

200g (7oz) crunchy, unsweetened peanut butter

350g (12oz) icing (powdered) sugar, sifted

80g (2¾oz) dark (bittersweet) chocolate , broken into pieces

good pinch of coarse sea salt (optional, but recommended!)

MAKES 30 SMALL SQUARES

Line a 20cm (8in) square cake tin with cling film (plastic wrap) or baking paper.

To make the fudge, melt the butter in a large saucepan over a high heat. Stir in the brown sugar and milk. Bring to a boil and boil for 2 minutes, without stirring. Then remove from the heat, and stir in the peanut butter. Put the icing (powdered) sugar in a large mixing bowl, then pour the hot peanut butter mixture on top and beat until smooth.

Pour the fudge into the lined cake tin, cover the top with plastic wrap or baking paper, and smooth the top. Allow to cool slightly for 10 minutes, then chill to cool completely. Once cool, remove the top layer of plastic wrap or baking paper.

Melt the chocolate in a bowl over a pan of simmering water, or in a microwave on its lowest setting. Spread a thin layer of chocolate over the fudge. Allow to set, then sprinkle the top with a little coarse sea salt, if using.

Using the plastic wrap or baking paper lining, carefully lift the fudge out of the tin onto a board and cut into about 30 squares. Store in an airtight container.

Index

Acknowledgements & Thank You's

First up, thank you to Pipers Farm, Isle of Wight Tomatoes, Microplane, ProCook and Aabelard Aprons who all generously donated food and equipment for the book shoot. Lou Archell of Little Green Shed, thank you for letting me ransack your kitchen and hot-foot it with a crate full of crockery.

Roz and Marc, for your big, bright kitchen. Of all the families who could cope with a book shoot team, and all that follows in its wake (online shopping deliveries, props, cameras, backdrops and people, lots of people) turning up every morning and before the kids have even left for school, it's you!

My friends (you know who you are) for cast-iron friendship and scooping of children up and off my hands when deadlines were looming. Also, for cooking some of these recipes and texting me an '*everyone loved it*' so soon after suppertime.

Sarah Lavelle, it's been a pleasure to work with you again on this book. I love that you let me write the book I want to write but, come crunch time, you absolutely know how you want the book to be. As creative processes go, it feels organic and dynamic, and refreshingly normal too.

Nikki Ellis for the design process, another corker. Likewise, Andy Mosse: I can't thank you enough for your beautiful drawings, what a privilege it is to have them in the book.

Sam Folan and Faye Wears; shooting this book was a blast. And hours of Spotify was enjoyed by all (was it not?).

And finally, the best bit of all. Matt, I wouldn't be the cook I am without you. Grace, Ivy and Dorothy, I love cooking for you and I always will.

All recipe feed 4 people unless otherwise stated.

Publishing Director Sarah Lavelle
Design Manager Claire Rochford
Designer Nicola Ellis
Photographer Sam Folan
Prop Stylist Faye Wears
Home Economist Matthew Williamson
Production Director Vincent Smith
Production Controller Nikolaus Ginelli

Published in 2019 by Quadrille, an imprint of Hardie Grant Publishing

Quadrille
52–54 Southwark Street
London SE1 1UN
quadrille.com

Cataloguing in Publication Data: a catalogue record for this book is available from the British Library.

Text © Claire Thomson 2019
Photography © Sam Folan 2019
Design © Quadrille 2019

ISBN 978 1 78713 254 2

Printed in China